Slum
Lord

By Arthur Richard Keim

And

Jeanette Stearns Keim

Copyright © Jeanette S. Keim

All about Art

Art Keim was no ordinary guy. His Slum Lord adventures were just one part of a lifetime of remarkable experiences that most people only hear about but never experience in their own dull world.

Art started out life orphaned as an infant during the depths of the great Depression. As a youngster, Art's tyrannical grandfather took him in, taught him how to work selling bootleg hooch to the Mafia, how to shine shoes on the streets of lower Manhattan—and how to charm the ladies. On his own he learned to entertain a crowd by dancing for tips before he was six years old.

A real-life Daddy Warbucks discovered this unusual child and took him on to raise. That's exactly what happened. This is no fairy tale. Art, the former orphan and street urchin, suddenly found himself groomed to fit into New York high society, complete with private tutors, fancy boarding school, weekends at the Met, the ballet, the Guggenheim and the Yacht Club. This was not a Hollywood make-believe story, but a real-life experience.

Life became complicated for Keim. He served in the Korean Conflict. He ended up, somehow, in Texas and got married. Society shifted. He was not intimidated by bureaucrats, academia, left wing socialists, petty know-it-alls, and what he saw as the infiltration of traditional standards of freedom.

How did so many changes affect him? Somehow he grew up with a unique, unforgettable character, and a personality that attracted people's attention and affection. Every event in his life—the good and the bad—was character building. He learned and practiced trust in himself, trust in God, loving people, and loving his country. Art was a man of courage and action.

Art was distinctly NOT an ordinary person. His escapades were many. Fearless, he met challenges, winning some and losing some, without regret.

Slum Lord? Yes he was, according to the ruling authorities; a benevolent Landlord according to his tenants, his associates in business, and those who knew him. This was only one of many conflicts he managed to survive.

This is a true story. It will make you laugh. It will make you proud.

Enjoy!

Disclaimer from Art:

This story, this book, is a collection of memories, with many of those memories from my childhood where I recall actual facts, dates, and reality are as truthful as I can remember. My recollections may not be absolutely precise, but they are exactly as I perceived reality at the time. I am also an opinionated person and my perspectives within this book about events, people and politics are often exactly that—my opinions.

Acknowledgements from Art and Jeanette (the scribe).

To Marvin Bahnman, our forever friend from Trinity Terrace, Fort Worth, Texas, who encouraged me to document Art's life story. Thank you Marvin. You gave me the spark to do it. Otherwise, this story would never be known and would never have a chance to inspire others. Thanks, Marvin, for your great skills at organizing, researching, bringing history to light, and getting things done. This story only happened because of you. Your gentle encouragement, your kindness, perseverance, and wisdom made it happen.

To Nico Van Thyn, our friend from Trinity Terrace, a professional sportswriter and author of "Survivors, #2511, #70726, Two Holocaust Survivors from Amsterdam to Auschwitz to America," the moving story of your own parents. It's your style of writing, your personality, and your energy that I have always admired. You were my inspiration to write Art's story. May God bless you for honoring your parents by documenting their story so that we must never forget.

Thanks as well to Melissa Stewart and Bea Van Thyn for sharing their two heroes with us. We are surrounded by a great cloud of saints.

"SLUM LORD" AUTHOR JEANETTE KEIM (LEFT), DRESSED IN FORMAL BLACK BEFORE A PIANO PRESENTATION. JEAN, JEAN, THE PIANO MACHINE IS STILL PERFORMING TODAY.

BELOW: ART AND JEANETTE'S FESTIVE CHRISTMAS CARD ART FROM A TRIP TO SANTA MONICA, CALIFORNIA IN 2010.

Preface

From the first time I met Art at a dinner party, we fell in love. Being very cautious about "love," thank God I didn't lose my head and do something stupid. I knew about bad boys. He was the perfect candidate, charming, movie star looks, out to get what all men want, the kind to break a girl's heart in a heartbeat. Not my heart!

Now I was in crazy love, yet there was something more, much more I needed to find out about him, and I did. A surprise awaited me. He was guileless. No putting on airs. No pretense. No cover-ups.

He was and is for real. I learned all about his orphaned childhood, his fractured family, his surviving the ghetto, his Daddy Warbucks, his romp with the New York jet set, his distaste for college, his playboy life. Nine months later I married him anyway. I learned his life's experiences made him what he is. It's a remarkable story. I was an eyewitness to the past 63 years of Art's life, including his time as an alleged Slum Lord. I saw that part firsthand. This hard-working, red-blooded American morphed from landlord to slumlord quite unintentionally.

I often remarked to Art that his story needed to be told. He was not anxious to think about the past, much less write about it. Finally, he agreed to a collaboration. He would tell it, and I would write it.

So now, dear readers, prepare yourself for one of the strangest, most amazing, and bizarre true-life stories you will ever read. It is my hope that Art's character will be an inspiration to you and others.

Here is that story....**Jeanette Stearns Keim, 2020**

Slum Lord Contents

Slum Lord

Part 1: Daily Life of a Slum Lord

"Rent's due, Harry," I told him.

It was a late Saturday night, and I knew Harry had money. His three scabby buddies glared at me, but Harry didn't look up from dominoes on the table. I didn't say anything else. But it was clear the request didn't resonate well.

After a long, hard minute he mumbled under his breath, "You're disturbing my game. Come back tomorrow."

The three thugs hardened their stares and one reached down to his knife scabbard on his hip. The other two crossed their fat tattooed arms. Clearly they were not sympathetic to a landlord's never-ending but always difficult mission: Collect the rent. Somehow.

"Rent's past due, Harry," I repeated. "I want my money now."

Harry barely looked up and said, "You better go now, Mistah Art, there ain't no rent money tonight."

There was a wad of big bills on the table. One thug began shuffling the bones, all face down. I walked closer to the table. The shuffling stopped. I paused a second and said, "Box cars," and turned over a domino. A double six looked up at us.

Before they fully comprehended what had just happened, I was out the door with the wad of past due rent money. Just another day in the life of a slumlord. Next week, next month, I'd be at it again.

I wrote this story for those who want to know more about the landlord industry, which some might refer to as the slumlord business, or for that matter much of it applies to any other red-blooded capitalistic American enterprise. Hopefully my experiences may give a boost of courage to many.   Others may decide that being a self-employed businessperson is not for them.   Since I, by nature, was never inclined to sit at a computer, I asked my good wife, Jeanette to do the writing. As I dictated my musings and recollections, she became the faithful scribe. She also is my witness to these accounts, which God knows is the truth.

It never occurred to me as a young man that I might turn out to be a landlord, much less a slumlord, as I journeyed down life's road. How I got there sort of evolved from other situations that I didn't plan on, but that's how things turn out sometimes. Circumstances and destiny alter our priorities. Our property and rent houses were close together, which is a great asset for anyone in the rental business.

How it happened requires a back story: Jeanette's parents lived in an old neighborhood that saw its heyday before World War II broke out.   The homes in this aging neighborhood were mostly big Victorian monstrosities devoid of modern conveniences like air conditioning or indoor plumbing, or at least indoor plumbing that consistently worked. It was a neighborhood in transition.

Original families had either died off or moved to the suburbs by the time I came around in the late 1950s.

The Stearns house was built by Jeanette's grandfather in 1905. The elder Stearns came to Texas from Ohio to seek his fortune as a plumber around 1890ish. He knew how to install a sensational new modern convenience claiming to be an instantaneous hot water heater. He was successful in selling these contraptions to the big cattle and oil barons for their mansions. And, being a good looking, smooth-talking Yankee, he was both savvy and charming, so much so that he was able to marry a local southern belle named Minnie.

The only problem was that Minnie's father was a former Confederate soldier from Tennessee who lost everything during the Civil War. Like many displaced Southerners, he went west, in his case migrating to Texas with nothing in the way of assets but his Confederate uniform, his wife and four daughters. They were dirt poor, but proud, and put on the airs like they were still rich folks, never conceding that the war was over.

The family's greatest prize of all was the beautiful Minnie, and she up and ran away with a YANKEE!

Minnie's Daddy never got over it. Never accepted it.

He sat on his front porch with a shotgun. Stearns was not allowed to set foot on his property. When the old gentleman died, he was buried in his cavalry uniform, sword and all, and he had a Confederate marker on his grave. Not long after his death, Stearns suddenly became ill with a fast-growing cancer and died quite unexpectedly. He left Minnie behind with a flock of little ones and the big house that he built in 1905. The family was totally unprepared for a second burial so soon, and not knowing anything better to do, they buried Stearns next to the family patriarch.

Minnie stayed in the big house with her oldest son, Harry Stearns, my wife Jeanette's father, but the younger children were farmed out to relatives. Harry, the son, finally gained ownership to the house, and many years later it finally, at long last, it went to Jeanette.

That's where I came in, landlord-wise.

Jeanette and I were already married. Somebody had to maintain the property, which was a total nuisance and not to my choosing. So marked the beginning of my years as a landlord.

At least I had skills in jerry rigging. In those days in Caucasian-speak, it was called "nigger rigging," not a racially appropriate term at all, but meaning the ability to fix things without spending any money (or as little as possible), this cheapskate process also knowing what to do and somehow getting the job done in a timely manner.

And with that, my new career was about to take off.

Old Mr. Gibson, who lived next door to the Stearns' house, made me an offer to buy his residence and other properties nearby. He was settling his affairs on his death bed, and none of his lazy nincompoop heirs wanted to be bothered with his ratty old estate in a crumbling neighborhood. How could I refuse? It seemed like a sweet deal. The price was right, and I said yes. In quick time I'd become owner and caretaker for four properties, all of them costing me money but with none of them generating

4

any income. It was definitely time to either get busy or go broke.

I began working on one property that had been a fine house in its day. It had marble mantles, huge solid wood sliding doors with lovely brass hardware, high ceilings, and spacious rooms. My plans were to convert it into a fourplex, the immediate cash-flow problem being that I would need to borrow some money to get started. Simple enough? Not.

The bank had a red circle around the whole neighborhood —eventually it would be called red lining—which meant no possibility of a loan deal, period. Now what? Before I could even scratch my head trying to think, the city code enforcement office sent me a certified letter saying I had thirty days to demolish the house or be fined $300 per day. I didn't realize it at the time, but in short order I had been introduced to the biggest and most formidable enemy to landowners—the city and its army of regulatory bureaucrats.

What to do? What to do!

The land was worth something since it was on a busy thoroughfare. Maybe I could rent it out for a used car lot, so I decided on demolition. I did it by myself, starting at the third-floor attic and working my way down. It was kind of fun but disheartening at the same time. I really felt trapped with no other options. Was the bank somehow in cahoots with the city? This had been a grand structure in former times, now a sad victim to the crowbar and the sledgehammer.

I salvaged a few things each day by lining them on the curb with a "for sale" sign: Some stained-glass windows, then a couple of non-working crystal chandeliers. While she was on break from the Merchant Marine Academy, my daughter Mildred and I helped a rancher load the hardwood floors to build a barn. By working 16-hour days non-stop, I barely finished before the deadline. The city won that bout, but there would be many more. I now had an empty lot, some very sore cracked ribs from falling through a second-floor balcony to the ground, and a swiftly evolving less-than-friendly attitude toward the city.

The planning and zoning commission was my next battle, which I didn't expect. I filed a routine request for a permit to open a used car lot. The property was on a busy street and adjacent to other business property, the telephone company, and a restaurant called the Chicken Shack. At the hearing, much to my surprise a bunch of long-haired, barefoot hippies showed up opposing my request! They represented an organization that I had never heard of, ACORN, an initialized acronym for the Association of Community Organizations for Reform Now.

Their smooth-talking spokesman appealed to the judge that the area served as low-income housing for the poor and needy, and further alleged I was a ruthless landowner out to make a profit on the backs of the homeless and downtrodden. That charlatan quack made me look like a greedy cold-hearted villain. The truth is I am sympathetic to the poor and needy, and this idiot was tainting my true character in court.

Honestly, at the time I was caught off guard, but God was with me, and I kept my cool, even though I wanted to strangle the hippie jerk on the spot in front of the judge. He came from out of nowhere, but I never forget a face. When our paths cross again and they will (I hope), this lowlife will get his due. He's a marked man.

My request was denied, so, by then growing desperate, I had to think of something else to bring in revenue. The hospital district was building a big addition to the community hospital nearby, and several adjacent homes were condemned and demolished for the land space. I made a deal (it was probably illegal) with somebody who I have now forgotten and found a salvation: I arranged to have a cute little brick duplex moved to my empty lot. The duplex was free for the taking, but I paid a house mover to do the job. He took every brick off the house, moved the house in the middle of the night, (also probably illegal) and put all the bricks back on.

The big house was gone. That's probably what riled up ACORN. For some unknown reason the city failed to condemn the servant's quarters in the back, which I had left standing. The little brick duplex fit perfect up front. With no financial help from the tight-ass bank, I scavenged all kinds of materials from paint, furniture and plumbing fixtures, converting the servant's quarters into two units, upstairs and down. Now I had four rentals, which got occupied remarkably swiftly. It was clear there was a market. Harry, the previously mentioned dominos gambler, moved in upstairs.

Harry was tough and I knew it. So were his domino playing henchmen. I just had to be tougher, that's all. I had plenty of tenants just like them. I could have started a revolution with those guys. They liked to fight, and it didn't matter whose side they were on. It made me sad when Harry moved away. Colorful people make the world a far more interesting place.

Harry's live-in girlfriend got raped in the neighborhood car wash. They didn't have a car.

Many well-intentioned people don't have the balls to be a landlord. Being good at managing property and taking care of business details is okay, but it's the tip of the iceberg. The bottom line is people skills. You're dealing with the public, and the public is very smart, smarter than the dimwitted condescending bureaucrats will ever know. Survival of the fittest is human nature, and every tenant in the world is out for himself or herself. The public knows how to screw the government, cheat on taxes, skate their bills, and con senile judges. The landlord is up against a multitude of socially accepted hurdles. He is an independent, single-handed, dirty word property owner collecting what is rightfully and legally due, the rent. Somebody's got to do it. But it's not for the fainthearted. There may be no such thing as a free lunch—or free rent—but a lot of tenants keep hoping this will become so.

My friend, Andrew, owned an apartment building across the street. He was polite, clean cut, and he drove a nice new pickup truck. His tenants always owed him money. Sometimes, lots of money. He died of a heart attack at age 48 sitting in his new pickup truck.

You need to know what you're getting into. What I'm relating to you, you don't get in a classroom. It's not what any professor teaches in school. The mealy mouth real estate 101 professors know a lot of theory, but most never really owned a rent house. Just ask them. If they did and were successful, they wouldn't be low salaried professors. Hands-on experience is what counts. There is money in it if you have the temperament. Look at Donald Trump. Remember, you must be tough. You must take the licks, and you absolutely must never hesitate to give out a few of your own. My properties, once located in the silk-stocking part of town in bygone times, found itself in the banks' redline as it evolved and slowly morphed into an inner city red light district, very close to becoming a slum. Along with the fading neighborhood I morphed into a slumlord.

Sob stories, lies, and fabrications beyond belief, flow like the flooding Mississippi every time a tenant opens his mouth, at least when the rent is past due. It's part of the game. You must let them shed their tears—think of this as providing therapy—while you keep a poker face but in the process turning off your ears. But then here's the rule:

 Don't leave until they've paid something. I didn't always get all my money, but my collections ran about 90 percent, good going for a slum lord. You must catch them on payday before they hit the bars. You must know when the government checks come in the mail, when the mail is delivered, and sometimes even be there to drive the tenants to the bank. Low rent residents pay in cash. They don't have bank accounts. Nor do they have credit cards, or at least they don't have cards that aren't already maxed out.

Evictions are a big problem, mainly because it takes so long to do it the legal way. The court system favors the tenant, which means they end up with more free rent days. So, I came up with my own system to get them out faster. It was perfectly illegal, but most of the non-payers were in trouble with the law already, so they usually wanted to stay away from the courts and the police. In all my years, I never once evicted a tenant who was down on their luck and desperately needed a place to stay. However, I put lots of chiselers and cheats who owed me money out on the street because they deserved it.

My own system? I had several. But Rosie, my pet rattlesnake, always worked.

One eviction was especially significant. This red headed guy with a ponytail rented Harry's old upstairs apartment. There was something about him that put me on alert, but I didn't know exactly what. Sure enough, when the rent came due, he refused to pay. After my third attempt to collect he still refused to pay and didn't make any excuses. I waited till he left, and I took off the front door. This always got rid of the drug dealers who didn't want anybody snooping inside their premises. With the apartment wide open I thought he would leave on his own. Well, he didn't. I was painting next door, and he comes dragging in and goes upstairs. It's the middle of the day. I called Jeanette and told her to drop everything and come over, which she did. I stationed her and Chainsaw, that was her dog, in the driveway to be my look-out. I went up the steps without a sound, baseball bat in hand. There he was, asleep on the bed. I let out a war whoop and banged him hard on the bottom of his feet.

He jumped straight up from a dead sleep. I grabbed him by his red ponytail, shoving him out the open doorway. I shoved him again, this time down the stairs. I was right behind him with the bat but didn't need to use it. He fell down most of the steps, got up and tried to run on the gravel driveway barefooted. He suddenly stopped staggering and hopping on one foot. He turned around and yelled up to me, "Can I have my boots?"

From the top of the stairs, I picked his goat ropers up and threw them as hard as I could, banging him on the top of his head. Jeanette started yelling like a Banshee, "Don't hurt him, don't hurt him!" I wanted to throw the bat at her.

The creep scrambled up the cyclone fence along the driveway. Chainsaw took a bite out of the seat of his underpants as he rolled over the top. He landed in the Chicken Shack dumpster next door with only his bloody underpants and his roper boots that I had so graciously returned to him. He must have made a call inside, because soon a big black limo with tinted windows picked him up. There was nothing in the apartment, so I put the front door back on while Jeanette kept watch. I knew I would see that red headed bastard again.

Me, I am a good guy in a way the street people understand. I wear work clothes, usually dirty by the end of the day, and as this book was being written driving a 1969 Chevy solid metal pick-up with a 350 V8 engine, tommy lift, heavy duty shocks, multiple dents, and three colors of paint. I kept heavy duty tires on it and always kept the engine well serviced. It doesn't look like much, but the assortment of paint colors confuses eyewitnesses. Jeanette calls it "Piece of Junk." Well, I love Piece of Junk almost as much as I love Jeanette. In fact, Piece of Junk saved my life one time when I was collecting rent.

The gang bangers living in the north duplex were giving me static about paying up. Since I wasn't about to leave empty handed, one of the sneaky little criminals pulled a knife on me. I dodged and ran out the door to the street faster than an Olympic track star. They were right on my tail. I stayed low and started up Piece of Junk. In her unpredictable but frequent way she backfired

Pow Pow Pow Pow Balooey!

The gang bangers must have thought I had a bazooka, because they disappeared in several directions like the cockroaches that they were. I didn't get my money that night, but I did get home for supper in one piece.

There was only one time in twenty years that we had one hundred percent occupancy. It lasted about a week. The rest of the time people were moving in and out, going to jail, sometimes fleeing to Mexico. It was almost like running a by-the-hour hot sheet hotel. I always collected security deposits in advance and rarely ever had to return them. Sometimes families vanished, leaving behind a house full of stuff, especially stuff from the charities, like TVs, canned goods and baby clothes. One time a family disappeared in the heat of summer. After two weeks, I entered their apartment, which had to be over 100 degrees, and found a dead rabbit in a cage and a half dead kitten that survived by drinking water from the toilet. Both animals had exact same black and white markings. Weird! I took the kitty home and Jeanette named him Pinto. He fattened up and grew into a beautiful long-haired Persian. We loved him, even though poor Pinto was a total feline neurotic. His first family never came back.

The Mexicans always had big families, lots of ninos. One Christmas I threw a party for all my tenants at the International Lions' Club meeting house in the neighborhood. We filled the place up with mamas, mamacitas, abuelas, tias, ninos, ninas, lots of muchachos and muchachas, but no hombres. Not one father showed up, maybe because we didn't serve cerveza. We had a big Christmas tree with Santa, baby Jesus in the manger, mariachis, turkey and dressing, cranberry sauce, tamales, Coke, pan dulces, you name it. Every kid took home a bag of new jeans, oranges and a toy.

A few days later one little smart mouth asked Jeanette when we were going to have another party. She told him, "You have a party next time and I'll come to your house."

The illegals, the drug dealers, and the prostitutes, I could deal with, but the city was always my biggest headache. The code enforcement officers prowled the streets looking for any excuse for a violation. I had stacks of tickets for frivolous infractions. I appeared so many times in court that the judge, who was Hispanic, finally looked the other way and usually let me off without a fine.

Then I got a certified letter from the city with a familiar tone like before; a big single-family dwelling was declared substandard, and I had 30 days to demolish it or be fined $300 per day. I had to relocate a family of twelve and decide what to do next. It was a sturdy house with historical features, and I didn't want to tear it down even though it was something of an eyesore. To restore it would have cost a fortune. What to do! What to do! Then I hit on an idea. I would put an ad in the newspaper and give it away to anybody who would move it. That's what I did, and it worked. The house was saved and got moved to the country.

Would you believe, it happened again. Another damn certified letter from the city. Demolish or get fined. This was a large single-family dwelling built in 1909, a house I had purchased from old Mr. Gibson. It was dilapidated, and when I started fixing it up to rent, I remember finding some old junk under the house including a blow torch, a coffin, and a machete. This time an investor with deep pockets answered my ad. The rescued old mansion was moved to a lake and turned into a bed and breakfast.

My troubles continued to escalate. A fourth certified letter arrived from the municipality notifying me to demolish an old relic on Jennings Avenue. By then I had become seized with an angry suspicion that something was just not right. The next day I really get hit with a bomb. A certified letter, this time from the Texas Historical Preservation Commission, stating that if I made any effort to destroy,

14

remove, or alter any structure in the newly designated historic district, specifically Jennings Avenue, I would be fined $500 per day. I didn't realize this, but I was caught in the middle of a power struggle between the city, which gave me the name Slum Lord, and the state of Texas. It was a battle between urban renewal and historic preservation.

I figured it was time to lawyer up.

A barrister named Sheldon agreed to take my case. He was an expert in real estate law, he grew up in the old neighborhood, and he liked me. We spent lots of time in court. In fact, I put him on retainer since I was giving him so much business. He had one absolute rule for me: Keep my mouth shut and let him do the talking. It was exceptionally wise advice.

I remember one particular court session I was there waiting—and waiting--at Sheldon's side, bored out of my gourd, when I looked up and walking across the hall in the back of the courtroom was that red-headed bastard that I threw down the stairs. This time he was in uniform and wore a badge. My mind raced. Was he a detective, a federal agent, a double agent,

a dog catcher? The worst in my book would be code enforcement officer. What was he doing here at City Hall! A fire in my gut raged. I could taste the smoke.

I told Sheldon, "I'm going to take a leak."

In the hall there the bastard was, standing by the fire stairs talking to a bunch of guys. He had his hand on the door like he was going to walk up. I ducked unnoticed into the elevator and got off on the floor above. I waited in the fire stairs. Sure enough, he started up the stairs, and it was my good fortune that he was alone. I met him on the landing. Before he could focus his eyes, I had him pinned against the wall and banged his head a few times.

"Badge or no badge, if you set foot in my 'hood, you're a dead man," I said. Then I threw him down the rest of the stairs.

"You still owe me two months' rent," I said, just in case he forgot.

Then I walked back to the elevator, but before I went down to the courtroom I ducked into the men's room. It was crowded. I did a U-turn and came out again. The porter was at the door sweeping.

"You sure keep this place clean," I told him as I handed him a five.

I slipped in next to Sheldon. "You weren't gone long," he commented. "Naw," I said, cool as a cucumber. What was that all about? I now had two witnesses to my whereabouts for the past five minutes.

Sheldon earned his money. He kept me out of jail and avoided big fines. After an eternity of court hearings, court appearances, court trials, court decisions and court appeals, I think he finally wore them down. One day he called me and said it was over. The city relented. All charges were dropped officially. It cost me thousands, but the victory was sweet.

I remember looking out Sheldon's 39th floor office window, savoring the long-awaited relief. Through the green landscape I saw the roof of Jeanette's old home place. I saw my other properties (some were now vacant lots where I had to get rid of the houses). I still had a few rental units left but now they were part of a newly designated historic district, which might be a good thing, maybe. It struck me that maybe my slumlord days would lighten up. Maybe. In a fleeting moment my eyes noticed a big curl of smoke. I saw the taillights of the firetrucks racing down Jennings Avenue. Wonder what's up? Then I forgot about it and congratulated Sheldon again on his success.

When I got home, Jeanette told me someone had set a mattress on fire at the big house on Jennings Avenue. It burned a hole in the roof. The CITY fire marshal roped off the house and told the tenants that they had to evacuate. Instead of celebrating, my evening was spent finding somewhere for four families to stay till I could repair the damage. There was a lot of water damage.

Slowly but methodically we eventually sold everything. Through the years the whole neighborhood changed and is still changing. There is plenty of run-down real estate still standing, but many, many properties are improving. New houses are being built to resemble the same architecture as the old houses that were demolished.

And finally. there was what I considered an act of God: Two buyers who love doing historic restorations bought us out.

I have great memories of those hard-working days as landlord. It might have been easier if I had accepted tenants with government rent assistance from programs like HUD's Section 8. I did try it a time or two, but the stiff regulations for the property owner were next to impossible to abide by, at least for my old relics. Accommodating modern building codes would have bankrupted a rich man. Demolish and start over was the city's preferred approach.

Regretfully, I never had the pleasure of settling the score with the agitator from ACORN. If our paths had crossed, I might well have done something homicidal, and Sheldon would have been back on my payroll. The slimeball never showed up again in the neighborhood after harassing me and defaming my character in court. I think he was a professional itinerant who

traveled around the country stirring up trouble. The organization stuck around but eventually collapsed from its own internal corruption. ACORN filed for Chapter 7 bankruptcy in November 2010.

A few years after I no longer owned any property except my homestead in the country, I received a certified letter from the city. It looked familiar. The city informed me that I had 30 days to demolish a substandard structure on Jennings Avenue or be fined $300 per day. I sold that particular address to the Veterans' Administration years ago. At that time the VA turned it into a parking lot. Now I was getting a nasty threat from the city about property I hadn't owned in years.

My blood boiled. The fire dragon inside me screamed the battle cry. I called Sheldon. He let me rage for a good five minutes before he interrupted.

"Calm down, Art," Sheldon said. "No need to worry. You know we're dealing with a bunch of Neanderthals. He laughed and hung up.

QUIPS FROM ART: Art to the CEO of Radio Shack, who is in the back of a long checkout line at the grocery store: "Hey Lenny, I'll sell you my space in line for five bucks!"

Jeanette Stearns Keim grew up in this house above, as it is today, at 1419 Lipscomb Street near Hemphill Street, a neighborhood now being rediscovered and renewed.

Below: Art Keim was famed for his enthusiastic appreciation of the performing arts. His grandson, Russell Wooten, penned an illustrative example of Art at a New York Philharmonic performance at the Lincoln Center in New York City. See if you can find Art. Here's a helpful tip: Look upper right.

MARCH 1991

The following statement was made by Code Enforcement officer W. C.
Ables, city of Fort Worth on Saturday, February 23, 1991, around
11:30 a.m. at 810 Ingram. The statement was addressed to
Arthur R. Keim in the presence of _Bonnie Mata_,
eye witness.

I was cleaning on the side of the house
when I heard loud nosie calling
slum lord owner to my land lord.
Mr. Keim.

Bonnie Mata
tenant
810 Ingram
Fort Worth, TX 76104

In a loud belligerent voice he said to me, "When are you going to
get rid of all your houses?"

I told him to get off my property and he replied, "I could call
the police to have you arrested because you have a hammer in your
hand."

In the presence of my tenant he called me a "slum owner" and
accused me of not providing running water and sewege service to
my tenants.

21

Life Goes On - Till Gabriel Blows His Horn

My days of slum lording brought in a modest income for my family. I managed only property that we owned, which was in the old neighborhood where Jeanette grew up. As time went on, friends and neighbors asked me to maintain their property, mostly undeveloped lots that needed regular upkeep to ward off the city code enforcement vultures.

The code enforcement bureaucrats would actually take a tape measure and measure the length of a grass blade to write up a citation if the length was an inch in violation. I stayed ahead of the city guys and, with no surprise citations, kept property owners happy.

And no, this was absolutely not the kind of career I dreamed about, but I didn't mind the hard work, long hours, or the sleazy people I dealt with.

I note that property management and rent property investments were not the first option in our married lives. Jeanette and I had a glamorous short-term career as ball room dancers when we first got married. For a couple of years, we lived in Hollywood, danced on several TV shows, did a lot of partying in Las Vegas during the "Rat Pack" days (Frank Sinatra, Joey Bishop, Dean Martin, Sammy Davis Jr. and Peter Lawford) and kept up with the jet set.

Then the glamour wore off and work became work.

Jeanette never liked southern California, finding it too cold, too pushy, too competitively cutthroat. She decided to return to school in Texas to finish up a degree, and I kept dancing. For a while. But it wasn't long until I packed up and went back to Texas.

We had saved up a little money, with which I bought a spanking new ice cream truck like I had seen up north. It was shiny new with "Freezer Fresh Ice Cream" outlined in bright lights, with a music box blaring loudly for the neighborhoods to know we'd arrived. It brought big smiles for everybody, their dogs and their children. I served soft ice cream, hot dogs, chili, chips and soft drinks. It was really the first food truck vending business to hit town!

Things were great for a couple of years. I bought a second truck, for which I was able to pay with cash. I had six push carts rigged with dry ice and six homeless men for employees. They walked the smaller neighborhoods ringing their bells until they sold out, came back empty and were paid on the spot.

Too good to be true? Unfortunately, it was.

One day the Restaurant Association decided I was cutting into their business and took me to court. The charge? I was disturbing the peace with the bells and music. I was keeping little children awake during nap time, and I was taking workers away from their work. They couldn't get me on sanitation violations. I kept those trucks squeaky clean with high marks from every Health Department inspection.

The court said I had two choices. I could reduce my selling hours to some ridiculous schedule that would make it impossible to keep help, much less make a profit, or I would be hit with a big fine and restricted to where I could sell. Not much of a choice but I continued to mull options over. But not for long.

The very next week one of my pushcart boys got robbed and knifed. He ended up in the hospital with a punctured lung. I decided it was time to liquidate. The sad part was letting my workers go. One of them was poor old Andy. He looked to be at least eighty years old, was skinny as a rail and no surviving teeth in his head. He was homeless, but he showed up for work every day and outsold everybody. He took it real hard losing his job. I managed to sell everything—trucks, carts, freezers, and inventory. I sold everything except Andy's cart. I gave it to Andy.

You would have thought I gave him a million dollars. Talk about gratitude! I thought he was going to smother me with hallelujah hugs and chewing tobacco kisses.

The only option for life after Freezer Fresh was evident. We had to start over. I operated a tote the note used car lot for a while, but my time was still tied up with the rent property. The car lot didn't work out, but suddenly I had my hands full maintaining other people's undeveloped property waiting to the sold someday. Sometimes we find opportunities, but also opportunities find us. Or they did for me.

As usual, nothing came easy.

The problem was vagrants taking up residence on the empty lots I maintained.

They put up tents and I pitched them in the street.

They hid in the bushes, so I cut down the bushes.

They set up camp sites. I demolished them with my tractor.

I managed to do all this when nobody was around, of course. Somehow by the grace of God I survived, but not without a few confrontations, broken ribs, licks and bruises, and numerous narrow escapes.

One incident really scared Jeanette when I came home bloody from knife wounds on my back and bloody face.

Here's what happened: It was a Sunday afternoon, hotter than Hades, and I was mowing old Dr. Kelly's vacant lot next to his office building. Out of the blue up walks this deranged nut, a big giant of a guy in his pajamas, who tells me to get off his property. I ignored him and kept on mowing. He turned and started walking away. After about ten minutes I thought he was gone. Next thing I knew he knifed me in the back. I whirled around forward, and he cut me across the face. I fell to the ground but before he knew what happened I pulled his feet out from under him. He fell to the ground backwards with eyes blazing. I jumped up and started stomping him. If my chainsaw hadn't been tied down in my truck I would have cut him up into a thousand pieces. I made sure I stomped his face a few more times, then I dragged his stinking body to the sidewalk and left him there.

Since I was bloody and not feeling too good myself, I drove home in Piece of Junk (Jeanette's name for my '57 Chevy work truck.) I drove very carefully since I didn't want to attract any attention. The angels must have gotten me home.   Jeanette took one look at me and started screaming. "I'm calling 911, I'm calling 911" she repeated over and over, and over and over.

"No, you're not. I'm okay. Now calm down and clean me up."

"You need stitches! And a blood transfusion, and a doctor to examine you," the hysterics got louder.

Now I had her to deal with. "You're not calling 911, no police, no doctor. Just clean me up."

My thought was I probably killed that guy and I didn't want to leave any kind of a trail. It did bother me, but I was suffering too, and I didn't want any more trouble.

Jeanette got me patched up and put me to bed. I hurt all over. Next day when I looked in the mirror and saw a beat-up face, fat lip, closed eye, big cut across my cheek. My aching back had a couple of big bandages.

I had to go back to finish Dr. Kelly's grass and that's what I did. Methodist Hospital was across the street, and I was friends with the security guard on duty. He came over to talk to me, but he didn't ask any questions. I guess my face told it all.

I asked him if he knew anything and he said, "Yeah, we found him near dead. He's in intensive care right now. He'll survive."

"Who is he, anyway?"

"He's an Alzheimer patient at the nursing home, a former Green Beret. They can't keep him locked up. He's been harassing the neighborhood for quite a while."

"So, he took quite a beating?" I asked.

"Yeah, and he deserved it. He's been a real troublemaker. He still had a knife in his hand when we found him."

My wounds gradually healed, but my face looked awful, purple black eye, big gash across my cheek. Jeanette and I had a trip planned with the art museum a few days later.

She wanted to cancel, but I said, "Let's go, and have a change of scenery." That's what we did. We took a bus trip to Chrystal Springs, Arkansas.

We knew several people on the trip, and it was good therapy for us to go. The first thing that happened when we got on the bus was that a couple from our church greeted us and Virginia asked in great surprise, "Art, what happened to you?"

"I got mugged".

Now everybody on the bus knew, and everybody in our 3,000-member church back home knew, because Virginia was on her cell phone immediately reporting the news.

On Sunday morning when we went to church, I was a celebrity greeted with "You got mugged!" So much for privacy.

The story of Agnes

The old neighborhood was changing, but for worse, not better. My mother-in-law, Agnes, still lived alone in the big house where we got married. She was in her nineties but still walked to the grocery store and did her own laundry outside on the porch in an old Bendix washing machine with a hand cranked wringer. I checked on her several times a week since I was around checking the rent property anyway.

Despite my efforts, she never liked me. I was a Yankee and raised Catholic, and I married her daughter. She never knew I got kicked out of the Catholic Church when I was a kid. I attended St. Mary's. My grandpa made me go, but he never went with me. They had a Boy Scout troop that I joined. Our scout master was a gay priest, not athletic and very effeminate. We begged and begged for him to take us camping, and his answer was always a firm, predictable "No."

Being a smart mouth street kid and tired of hearing the same old "No," I asked him in front of the whole troop, "Are you gay?" That was the end of my membership in that troop. They kicked me out, and I joined another troop sponsored by a non-English speaking Italian Methodist Church.

It was a scouting upgrade. They took us camping. We rode the subway to the George Washington Bridge, walked across the bridge, and then hiked five miles to the Boy Scout Campgrounds in Tenafly, New Jersey. We carried our pup tents, cooking utensils, bacon and beans and everything else we on our backs. Always had a great time!

Back to Agnes. We got a phone call from her early one morning. There was a bullet hole in the wall across from her bed. I told her I'd be right over to take a look. Sure enough, there it was just as she'd described; a bullet hole and the bullet shell lying on the floor. Weird! Next, I checked the window next to her bed, and there was another bullet hole in the glass. Apparently, the bullet came through the window, flew across the bed with her asleep in it, landing in the opposite wall. It must have missed her by an inch or two. She didn't seem concerned about it and I tried to keep it that way. She hadn't heard anything, slept all night, and called us to come and clean up the busted sheetrock and broken glass on the floor.

There were two other times she reported a problem. She claimed that she heard an intruder in the kitchen. She kept a baseball bat under the bed which she grabbed, and sure enough there he was, rummaging around in the refrigerator. She screamed bloody murder, swinging that bat (according to her) and he took off out the back door. Whether this was true or not—I couldn't tell for sure—we started to be concerned. She could scream like a Banshee warrior, and I did find a broken latch on the backdoor screen.

The other incident was about the same. This time it was a noise in the living room. Again, according to her, she surprised the intruder with her Banshee scream, swinging that bat. And yes, I did find the broken window glass and slit screen. It was time to think about moving her out.

There was another incident I mentioned earlier when her dog, Big Mac, chased a prowler over the fence. He ripped the seat of his pants out. That dog was just as brave, or I should say as it was just as mean, as Agnes. Her late husband called her "the barracuda." The police found the bad guy on the roof of a neighbor's garage nursing a bloody bottom, the seat of his pants missing.

We found a nice nursing home close by that would take Miss Agnes. She had zero health problems, and to our surprise she was willing to go without a fight. We were greatly relieved. God takes care of his own, her and us too.

When we got her settled in her new room at the nursing home, she looked out the window and remarked, "This is so nice. There's my church right across the street." It was the parking garage of Methodist Hospital.

The years passed, lots of them, and she began showing little signs of, as her doctor put it, "old age dementia." By then she was more than 100 years old. I visited her often, almost daily since I was working in the old neighborhood checking on the properties. When you have someone institutionalized, it's a good idea to keep your eyes on them on a regular basis. You never know what can happen.

I stopped by one afternoon and they were putting Agnes in an ambulance. They told me she was where she was not supposed to be, had lost control of her wheelchair, flew down a ramp, fell out, ripped the skin off her hand, and who knows what else got injured. I followed the ambulance to the emergency ward and waited a long while. They checked her over and found nothing seriously wrong except the hand. She was in good spirits and asked for me. A kind surgeon met me and asked if I would like to watch the surgery as he sewed the skin back in place.

I peered at her skinless hand. The skin was still attached to her wrist but rolled up. It looked gory to me. What I saw in that skinless hand was exposed bones, muscles, and stuff I didn't recognize.

Agnes asked me, "What do you see?"

"I can see China." Everybody laughed. So did Agnes.

Thank God for the professionals. That young doctor sewed her up, and I took her back to the nursing home for supper. She never complained about anything.

When I got home, Jeanette did all the screaming and passed out.

On a later visit as I was leaving, Agnes said to me, "Art, are you still living with that woman?"

She had forgotten that I was married to her only child. Agnes didn't recognize her daughter, anymore. Jeanette visited her Mama every week, did her laundry, took her for "walks" outside in her wheelchair, took her to the ice cream socials every Friday, etc. etc. Then one day Agnes said to Jeanette "And who are you, my dear?"

"I'm Jeanette. I'm your daughter." Agnes looked puzzled, then replied in a cheerful voice, "I didn't know I had a daughter!" Strange how the human mind works or how it quits working. Agnes never liked me until her last days. Yet she forgot her own devoted daughter.

Remarkably, Agnes lived 106 years spread across three centuries: July 8, 1899 to April 15, 2005. When she died, she was taking only one medication, an appetite enhancer. She had natural brown hair when she died in her sleep. May she rest in peace with

Jesus, the angels, and her beloved ancestors.

QUIPS FROM ART: Leaving the doctor's office after a prostate cancer biopsy, Art announced to the crowd in the waiting room, "I've been snipped!" Then he turned to the receptionist, "How about a date?"

Charcoal portrait of Agnes drawn by Jeanette's second cousin, artist Keisha Leigh Smith

One of the famed Freezer-Fresh trucks...too sucessful for their own good

Austin Symphony Orchestra 1955

Jeanette , 19, playing cello for ASO

Art and Jeanette, dance instructors at Arthur Murray Studios, Pasadena 1958

Part 2

The Adventures of Little Orphan Artie:

How it began on the sidewalks of New York

Little Artie and Pop

Pop, which is what I called my grandfather, Evaristo Quinones, was a Spaniard from Andalusia. He worked with the bulls grooming and training them for the bull ring. He had the demeanor of a bull fighter, tall, thin, arrogant, proud, and fearless. When times got hard in Europe, Pop migrated to Puerto Rico, then to New York City, East Harlem. It was a real slumville with maybe 200,000 immigrant people crowded into ten acres of walkup apartments. English was not the first language.

There was no such thing as bull fights in America. West Texas had no market for mean bulls, and the cattle business was too far away, plus there were other ways to make a living. Pop didn't mind hard work. He had many skills, which made it possible for him to have many odd jobs, the most profitable one being the brewing of bootleg liquor for the Mafia. In addition to the great quality of his alcoholic product, he had the balls, the moxie to deal with a gangster-laden Italian underworld.

Being a handsome ladies' man also got him into lots of trouble. He ended up with far too many girlfriends, which then became too many wives, which then became too many children. Yes, too many, too many of all that. When his daughter died of tuberculosis, at age 29, she left behind an alcoholic husband and five little orphans.

The youngest orphan was me, little Artie.

All the kids were sent to an orphanage except the baby, who went to a hospital with mastoid problems. In those days before antibiotics, children with ear infections were treated with mastoid surgery behind the ears. The nurses fell in love with him because—so I'm told—he was so cute and full of personality, even with his head covered with white bandages that looked like a football helmet. That was me with all the bandages.

So goes the story as told to me by my cousin, Rita, Tia Ambrosina's daughter. That illness left me with scars behind my ears. There are gaps in Rita's remembrance, but I remember being cared for and loved by a big Italian family. The mother had big boobs and my favorite spot was to sit in her lap with my head resting on that gigantic chest. She rocked and sang to me, and we were happy together.

My only other memory of those times was when Santa Claus visited us at Christmas. Our foster mother shoed all the children out of the parlor while Santa put on his suit. I sneaked away and hid behind the curtains to watch Santa. He put on his red suit, then he did an unusual thing. He moved a corner of the couch from the wall, pushed his white beard to the side and spit out a big wad of chewing tobacco. As it trickled down the wall, he moved the couch back in place to cover up his deposit.

Nasty Santa gave a signal, and the children came running in laughing and falling over each other to sit on his lap. Not me. I refused to get near him. After he left our mother scolded me for not sitting on Santa's lap. I remember grabbing her hand and taking her to the couch. It was too heavy to move. The other curious children standing around watching helped, and together we moved that big heavy couch away from the wall. There it was! His nasty, ugly brown streak dripping down to the floor. I must have been three or four years old. Some experiences burn themselves into our memories.

Then one day a welfare lady took me to my new home, East Harlem apartment, a sixth-floor walkup at 204 E. 112th Street.

QUIPS FROM ART: Art to the executive director of Imagination Celebration, walking unannounced into her office, "Get off the phone Ginger, you need to talk to me."

Great Depression Christmas

By Jeanette Keim

The approaching Christmas season filled little Artie with that virgin wonder reserved for small children. With a trembling hand he held tight to his grandfather as they worked their way through the crowded streets of Manhattan. Fat bearded Santa's occupied every department store entrance ringing their bells, smiling, spreading good cheer. The sidewalks buzzed with busy people preparing for the special season.

Caught up in the fervor of Christmas, the young child forgot his shabby clothes and cold feet. The year was 1934, the depths of the Great Depression. Artie was lucky to have a home with his grandfather. His older brothers and sister were not so fortunate and were farmed out to orphanages. When their mother died in childbirth, none of the family members could afford to keep the siblings together. There were too many mouths to feed during hard times. The aunts and uncles had their own hungry families to fend for. Even sadder was the plight of the children's father. He grieved himself to drink over the sudden death of his young wife. Before long he lost his meager job, then he lost his children, one by one. Little Artie, the baby of the family, ended up with Pop and Ana. Pop, a proud Spaniard, brought Old World traditions with him when he immigrated to New York.

Their home was strict—too strict because the truth was that Pop was a tyrant.

Love and kindness barely found expression. The struggle for survival dominated their whole existence. Little Artie was not especially welcome in their humble home. He was a stranger, but they tolerated him, and the curly headed, beaming child brought sunshine and laughter where it had not existed before.

The Christmas before, Artie had his bad experience with a fat chewing-tobacco-Santa in the foster home. This year would be different. This was little Artie's first Christmas at

Pop's house. They had no tree with lights or decorations in their tiny apartment, but the city was beautifully decorated everywhere. Pop took Artie to see the big tree at Rockefeller Center, which must have been the most beautiful tree in the world. To the small child the city, and the scenes outside, were enough to fill his heart with the spirit of the happy, holy season. He loved Christmas. He loved the birthday of the Baby Jesus.

At church on Christmas Eve, they sang wonderful songs and saw the manger with Mary and Joseph, the three wise men, and the shepherds ready for the infant Jesus. Little Artie swelled with adoration when he heard the words ring out about peace on earth, good will toward men. Joy to the World, O Come all Ye Faithful. "Silent Night" was his favorite, especially the part about Christ, the Savior is born ... CHRIST THE SAVIOR IS BORN.

After the service they lined up and waited to see Santa Claus. This year's Santa was skinny! When little Artie's turn finally came, he was exhausted from the excitement of it all. His heart almost failed when skinny Santa gave him a red stocking filled with fruit and a peppermint candy cane.

"Merry Christmas, Santa." Artie remembered to say, his voice quaking with awe. Ana had coached him carefully.

The next morning Pop awakened his little grandson early. "Santa paid you a visit last night. Come and see."

The young child leaped from bed, shaking himself loose from happy dreams of Toyland, turkey and dressing, cranberry sauce, yuletide carols still dancing in his head.

Across the cold floor his bare feet flew into the front room where Ana was preparing hot cocoa.

On the table next to his Christmas stocking was a beautiful toy fire engine. Little Artie froze in his tracks. His eyes grew as big as Little Orphan Annie's.

"It's for you," his grandfather said. "It's your Christmas present from Santa."

Artie ran to the table to look at the shiny bright red fire engine. It had ladders and hoses and a miniature catching net. The firemen were dressed in boots and slickers just like the real thing. The child reached out his hand shyly, almost afraid to touch it.

"Go ahead, play with it," his grandmother urged him.

From that moment on Artie and the fire engine were inseparable. Fires were fought all around the apartment's small rooms. With great volume, Artie simulated siren sounds as the red engine raced to imaginary fires behind the couch, under the beds, under the table and between the chairs, in the hall; on the steps, Everywhere the little boy was allowed to play. When the Chrysler Building caught fire from a surprise attack of wild Mohicans, the tall ladders cranked up to the windowsill skyscraper to swiftly rescue the helpless occupants.

The General Slocum tragedy was Artie's favorite drama. Pop told the story many times. At the turn of the century a side wheel excursion steamer burned in the East River killing over 1,000 passengers, mostly German children going to a Sunday School picnic. Only in Artie's reenactment were the children saved by his heroic red fire engine that put out the fire on board. The heroics continued as the red engine plucked out drowning children from the dangerous waters with hooks, poles, ladders, and remarkable feats of imaginary bravery.

Artie loved his fire engine, his only toy. He had no other pastimes. No friends, no pets, no games. Pop and Ana's household was a somber place for a growing young boy full of energy and life. The fire engine was his only companion. He spent days in contented play, always together with his beautiful toy.

Ana and Artie were confined behind locked doors when Pop was at work. Ana didn't have much to say to the child, except to quiet him down when he made her nervous. They learned to like each other despite their natural differences. They were two strangers from two different eras, young Artie, the intruder, old Ana the imposed upon. Yet the bonds of family love and responsibility brought them together.

Sometimes after working-hours Pop would take Artie on his 'rounds'. They visited many wonderful places, restaurants, saloons, and neighborhood bars where Pop and the proprietors would do business together.

Pop's day job as Artie was told was in a large bakery. On the side behind locked doors at the tiny apartment he distilled home brew and sold it without the proper licenses. Though Prohibition was over, Pop continued his bootleg business. He made a good product. His only customer, the Sicilian Mafia, provided anything he needed.   When he ran short of supplies, the Italians managed to rob a delivery truck.

Pop's apartment was on the top floor of the tenement for a good reason.   The fumes and odors from the brewing booze went skyward so as not to arouse suspicion. Contraband deliveries of supplies were made via roof top from a vacant building next door.   In the dark of night, deliveries were made across temporary planks laid down between the two buildings.   The delivery men didn't mind the height.   They grew up rooftop jumping just like the adolescent boys growing up in high rise neighborhoods did in those days and still do.   The walk-up tenements were built five feet apart, six stories in height.   204 112th Street, New York NY, Pop's address.   The neighborhood of ten acres, mostly six story tenements, five feet apart, housed 200,000 residents.   Rooftop jumping was and, I'm told, still a rite of passage for teenage boys.

With elaborate contraptions spread over the house Pop brewed a fine absinthe.   Artie was told it was "cough medicine."   The Italian customers bought the stuff in large quantities. Hemingway mentions absinthe in his novel, "For Whom the Bell Tolls." Spanish guerillas used it as an anesthesia during WWI. It's made from wormwood oils and flavored with licorice (anise).

Outings with Pop were rare.   The little boys' existence didn't include much affection or attention, but he did have a roof over his head, rice and beans to eat, a red fire engine to keep him company, and jugs of "cough medicine" under his bed.   If he felt bad, like catching a cold, he would unscrew one of the jugs, dip in his finger, and lick it.   In a minute he was conked out, fast asleep. When he woke up the next morning, he felt fine.

One day Artie noticed that the leaves outside were changing color. Ana told him autumn was near. That is about the time a tragedy happened. The red fire engine disappeared. One morning it was gone! Artie searched the house over and over. He looked everywhere. He asked Pop and Ana to help him look. They didn't show much interest. The child was beside himself with worry. When he started to cry, Pop gave him a hard whipping. The child hid in a corner with his grief and stayed all day. He had nothing else to do.

Weeks dragged by, long and lonely for the little boy without a toy. The beautiful autumn leaves that he could see from his upper window blew away, leaving the trees bare. Artie knew how leafless trees felt, standing so straight and silent. He knew what it was like to lose something.

Pop was gone all day working but there was never any money. Times were hard. Even with his illegal liquor sales, it was difficult to make ends meet. The house was cold and drafty. Pop and Ana argued violently. Artie hid under his bed with the jugs during the sieges least he get hit by a flying pot or pan.

The grandparents mellowed as Christmas Day drew near. Their dispositions improved as though the spirit of peace and good will took effect temporarily. On December 24, 1935, Christmas Eve, the family went to church and saw the manger ready for baby Jesus. They sang carols together and heard the Bible story about the nativity. After the service a Santa gave all the children a stocking with fruit and candy. Little Artie was wild with joy when good Santa put him on his knee and wished him a Merry Christmas and Happy New Year.

The next morning Artie woke up as Pop called to him, "Wake up, sleepy head. Santa was here during the night."

The child leaped from his bed and dashed into the front room. There on the table where he left his Christmas stocking was a beautiful red fire engine!

Artie stopped in his tracks, not sure if he was awake of dreaming. This can't be true, he thought. I'm still asleep!

"It's your Christmas present, Artie," said Pop. "Go ahead and play with it."

The little boy came to life and ran to put the toy on the floor. It was exactly like his old one, only cleaner and shinier. The happy child counted the firemen. He raised the ladders. He uncoiled the hoses and rolled them back up. For the rest of the day, he played with his fire engine, completely absorbed in make-believe fires and rescues.

When the real sirens howled on the streets below, Artie and his fire engine raced around the apartment answering emergency calls with the same urgency and importance as the New York City Fire Department. Being a fireman is a responsible job, especially for a five-year-old boy.

Little Artie spent many happy months playing with his fire engine. He parked it in a special 'station house' under his bed. The tires began to show small signs of wear, a few scratches appeared as time passed, but the cast iron toy held up remarkably well to its rugged daily routine.

When late September rolled around, little Artie noticed the leaves starting to change color again. He remembered last year about autumn and how the leaves blew away and left the tree branches bare. The thought made him uncomfortable, but only for a moment. He had big fires to fight that day—the schoolhouse on the corner, Saint Bart's Cathedral, the shipyards, the statue of Liberty, and his most favorite rescue of all, the General Slocum and 1,000 drowning Sunday School children.

Artie occupied himself with his childish fantasies of fighting fires till it was bedtime. The engine got routinely parked in its station under the bed awaiting the excitement of tomorrow.

Then one morning the engine was missing. Again. The station under the bed was empty. Maybe I left it in the other room, the child rationalized, hoping his toy had been carelessly forgotten the night before. But he knew for sure that the engine had been parked in its station at bedtime. He was careful every night to put the engine safely under the bed, say his prayers, and jump into his covers with a comfortable feeling that his engine was nearby.

A quick look around the apartment left him sick with dread. The engine was nowhere to be found. Ana ignored him when he begged her to help him search.

"You left it somewhere, and it got stolen," she said. "That's all. I can't help it if you are careless with your silly toy."

Her cold words hit him like mortal blows. Despair swept over Little Artie as he realized the awful truth. Something was wrong. His engine was gone. All at once he was confused, hurt, grief stricken. The child burst into a fit of crying. His horrible loud screams swiftly brought on frazzled nerves and Ana's wrath. She gave him a hard whipping.

The gold and red leaves of autumn fell, and the cold wind blew them away, leaving the naked tree branches shivering in the wake of winter. The sad, lonely child watched from an upper window.

Pop took little Artie to see the Macy's parade again on Thanksgiving Day. The child thrilled at being there on the street among the thousands of happy children. Floats filled with fairyland scenes, dancing animals, story book characters, Santa and his elves, the reindeer, and a workshop full of wonderful toys delighted the crowds with dazzling wonder. Artie swelled with the magic of Christmas. He secretly hoped that good Santa would not forget him.

Times were tough. The family subsisted on a poverty diet of rice and beans. On rare occasions Ana prepared a bony chicken. Pop was always working but there wasn't much money. The home brew enterprise didn't seem to improve their situation.

Christmas Eve was like last year; church, the skinny Santa, the red stocking filled with two oranges, a big apple, and a stripped candy cane. When it was time for bed, the tired little boy placed his stocking on the table. He secretly wished for a Christmas toy in the morning, but he wasn't sure if the good saint would remember him. The baby Jesus was poor too, and he received presents. But he was a King from heaven. Little Artie didn't know what else to do but say his prayers and go to sleep with hopes that Christmas morning would bring a happy surprise.

Artie woke up to joyful sounds. Hark the Herald Angels sing, glory to the newborn King! Dashing to the front room where the music was coming from, he saw Pop and Ana full of smiles. Standing on the table next to his Christmas stocking was an almost new radio.

"Look what Santa brought for our house, Artie," Pop beamed. "Now we can enjoy music and the news."

It was a beautiful table model radio with a picture of a fox terrier on the label. Artie was astounded that Santa left such a big gift. His little face now beamed to see his grandparents smile and enjoy the holiday music.

"Look over here, Artie," Pop added as he pointed to the other side of the radio.

Artie ran around the table and grabbed a shiny fire engine in his skinny arms. He could hardly believe Santa left two gifts, one for the family, and one for him. His heart pounded with happiness.

Ana had the hot cocoa ready. Artie could hardly tear himself away from his new fire engine long enough to eat. The day passed pleasantly with wonderful music pouring from the radio. Ana prepared a chicken along with the rice and beans.

The floor became streets again; the furniture changed into giant New York City skyscrapers that broke out in raging fires. Explosions and disasters, billowing black smoke, and daring rescues keep Artie and his fire engine busy for many happy months.

Now he was five years old, and when autumn came he entered school. Adjusting to the big change in his life, he enjoyed going to Public School 102 every day. He welcomed the influence of the world outside. Still his playtime at home was spent with the wonderful toy he loved.

One evening during supper little Artie looked at his plate of rice and beans. He carelessly remarked, "I'd rather have a hot dog."

Before the words rippled from his mouth, Pop's hand swung across the child's face, knocking him out of his chair. He landed against the wall in a heap on the floor.

"¡No reclamas sobre la comida buena de Dios!" Pop roared in Castilian Spanish. "Don't you ever complain about God's good food!"

Too frightened to breathe, the terrified child kept his head low so that Pop wouldn't notice the tears that he couldn't hold back. Through blurry eyes Artie saw his engine turned over near the table where the chair fell. The head on one of the firemen lay in cruel shattered pieces.

Times were tough that winter. Pop was frantic to find a job. He and Ana quarreled till Artie thought they would kill each other. They still had the radio, but it babbled depressing news about the economy. President Roosevelt talked to the nation about some kind of "New Deal." Wonderful as the New Deal sounded, so far its effects had not trickled down to the common people on the streets who bore the suffering.

Like an ugly recurring nightmare, the fire engine disappeared again without explanation. One dreary day Artie came home from school to find his engine missing from its station house under his bed. The familiar hurt and confusion rained down upon the still unsuspecting child. Again, he cried bitterly over his loss.

On Thanksgiving Day 1937 Pop and Artie saw the annual Macy's parade on Fifth Avenue. As always, the great pre-Christmas parade lifted the child's spirits, and for a few moments he and throngs of other children were swept up in the wonderland of Christmas. Yet the nation floundered deep in Depression. Thousands of people were out of work. Many went hungry. Pop was unemployed. Artie's shoes pinched his toes, but there was no money to buy him pair that fit. Ana stuffed his ill-fitting shoes with cardboard to cover the holes in the soles.

As Christmas drew near, Artie instinctively lived the cheery spirit of giving and sharing. With a careful hand he fashioned Christmas cards for Pop, Ana, and his teacher using paper from his writing tablet and borrowed crayons. Neither the nation's gloom nor personal hardship dampened his exuberance for Christmas and celebrating Jesus' birthday.

On Christmas morning little Artie woke up to the strains of "O Holy Night" flowing gently from the radio. He leaped from his bed and dashed into the front room where Pop and Ana were drinking coffee. On the table next to his Christmas stocking Santa had left him a gift—a bright, shiny red fire engine!

With a joyful squeal he ran to the table to examine his beautiful new present. It smelled of fresh paint and had no dents or ugly scratches like the old one. Artie reached out to put the fire engine on the floor when he noticed the fireman in the driver's seat. His head was broken off.

Artie stiffened in surprise. Now he knew! The stunned child looked at Pop and Ana. In that frozen silent moment Artie wondered if they could tell that he discovered their secret. Maybe he had a secret now. They were watching him, their weary faces transformed with temporary smiles as they shared his joy. No other gifts were on the table that year, only the fire engine. The two cards Artie drew hung affectionately on the wall over the radio.

The young boys' attention returned to his beloved fire engine. He was a wiser child now. No words were expressed. Knowing the truth didn't really matter. He broke the silence and began the siren noises. Driving his Christmas toy around the room with a newfound dignity, Artie stopped at his grandparents' chairs. He gave Pop and Ana a warm kiss and wished them a very merry Christmas.

From Little Artie's view:

When I was six years old, I was introduced to my older brothers and a sister who I had never met. They ignored me. I figure I ended up there through the welfare, which probably meant Pop was paid to keep me and my siblings.

He had his hands full. My new sister, Mary, was nice. She helped Ana, Pop's current wife, with household chores. The three boys were dumb, lazy, useless, and ran away from home a lot. There were seven of us squeezed into a tiny sixth floor walkup apartment. Besides us, there were two dogs and an old parrot that talked, mostly cuss words. How did I fit in? Pop put me to work as his assistant. No joke! He had bad eyes, and my job was to read the thermometer on the bathtub still. I was preschool age but learned fast.

Then I had another job. When my dumb wayward brothers went missing, which was often, Pop, and I had to go chase them down. Again, Pop needed my good eyes. Chief, the 150-pound German shepherd guard dog, stayed home to protect the apartment, though in reality his job was to guard the still. Chief could stand on his hind legs and put his front paws on Pop's shoulders. Pop was six-foot-four.

As I grew older Pop taught me how to carry the half gallon jugs with my pinkie and index fingers, one jug on each hand down the six flights of stairs where a big black limousine waited for us. Each jug was inside a bag so that onlookers would not recognize what I was carrying. How did I do it? It was not brute strength, but something about balance and focus. I was around six years old. The Mafia supplied Pop with all the ingredients he needed. On delivery each clear glass jug was held up to a light to check for clarity. Then Pop got paid and we went home in the limo.

Pop and I would deliver the juice to their homes. By request from the wives, I always accompanied Pop. I played with their children and romped around among their big sea trunks full of cash. Nobody spoke English.

One day Pop got his own limo. No one asked where it came from. Probably it was the Mafioso who provided the limo. Now he had two jobs. Besides delivering the booze, Pop drove families to a state institution for the retarded in upstate New York. And yes, I went along too. My job was to entertain the riders and the residents after we arrived.

While Pop took care of business, I was on my own. Being a little kid, unbiased, and non-discriminating, I just had fun. On arrival I was immediately surrounded by downs syndrome patients of all ages, though back then we incorrectly called them mongoloids. In addition, there were those afflicted with mental handicaps, some of them nonverbal, the mix including the old, young, fat, skinny, all ages and descriptions. They knew me. We danced around, hoot and hollered, chased each other, and rode the whirly thing on the playground. I was the only one who knew how to push and make it go fast. When it stopped, the attendants always came rushing out and hosed the whirly thing down. The riders who soiled their pants got hosed down too. I considered it great hilarious fun to get hosed down!

The trips were always fun except for one unforgettable disaster. We got hijacked! We had a carload as usual. It was a cold winter morning. We were on a lonely stretch of road when a woman with a baby flagged us down. Pop stopped, which for him was a rare mistake! Three masked bandits jumped out of the bushes with waving guns. The female with the baby disappeared! They robbed every passenger including us. They took money, jewelry, gifts for the residents, anything of value, and left us empty-handed, only a few miles from our destination. I asked Pop why they didn't take the limo.

"Estupido! Los burros demasiado tontos para ponder conducir un coche. (Donkeys are too dumb to drive.)

Pop struggled to feed us. These were Depression days. These were tough times everywhere, especially in the ghetto. Sister's cooking was the same old same old, rice and beans, more rice and beans. The hot dog incident shut my mouth about complaining. That's when he knocked me across the room for complaining about the rice and beans.

I remember walking in parades down 1110th Street campaigning for Mayor Fiorello La Guardia. We marched in the snow, where my too tight shoes had holes in the bottom, the cardboard stuffing didn't keep out the cold or the wet. I really liked that little wop (okay, the little Italian), because he personally gave us, the marching street urchins, five-cent chocolate bars for marching.

One day I got up the courage to ask Pop for money to buy a candy bar. He didn't get mad. He didn't hit me. Calmly he said, "Artie, it's time for you to go to work." Next thing I know he presented me with a shoeshine box, fitted with shoeshine supplies. It contained everything I would need. Now I could make some money and buy my own candy bars, I thought. But...not exactly. The terms were simple: I had to turn in all my daily earnings to Pop. And I owed Pop for the shoeshine box and the supplies. It didn't matter. Now I could get out on the streets and make some money for a change!

I was around eight years old. In retrospect, it was too young to turn pro.

This was nothing I could do on my own. To be safe, Pop hooked me up with a little group of other shoeshine boys. We stuck together; shining shoes in the train stations, on the streets, and around big skyscrapers along Fifth Avenue until police would run us off.

We kept our boxes hidden in the underground bowels of the subway stations, so other gangs couldn't steal our stuff. We didn't think of ourselves as a street gang. We were just a group of youngsters, a clan of urchins trying to make a buck.

I slowly paid Pop off for my box. I figured out how to hold back a nickel or two to buy a candy bar. Pop took the rest of my money. Our group was nondiscriminatory multiracial: Jewish, Irish, Latinos, blacks, whatever. I was the youngest. My best friend was Mario, the oldest, the smartest, and the toughest. Though not full grown, he was built like a prize fighter.

We had fun, this little band of street brothers. The blacks and the Italians turned shoe-shining into dance, street dancing, and that's how we made the most money. We put on a great show, and made great tips, more money than shoe shining. For me, this was life changing.

Dancing is in my soul. I've been dancing ever since.

Mario also carried a switch blade knife. Our time together had a bitter encounter that I will never forget so long as I live. He and I had put away our shine boxes in the subway station hideout and headed for home on foot. It was late and the streets were spooky dark. From the shadows of a doorway a nude man appeared wagging his fat penis.

"Let's play, boys," he said.

Mario grabbed my arm but didn't say a word. We picked up our pace.

"I mean it, pricks," the nude man barked.

Before I knew what happened, the pervert jumped at us— he screamed, staggered and fell to the ground. Mario had knifed him in the scrotum before I could blink an eye. We took off running. We finally reached a streetlamp, stopped a minute to catch our breath, looked at each other silently, and walked on home. Silence is the code of the streets. Nothing more would be said of the incident.

I was around nine. Mario was maybe thirteen.

A year or so later I remember a citywide strike that turned bloody. The union truck drivers and delivery men went on strike and refused to deliver the newspapers. Business was coming to a halt. I'm not sure how it happened but I rounded up my shoeshine brothers to sell papers for the New York Daily News. We stationed ourselves at the four corners of 42nd and Broadway and sold the Daily News.

The police always showed up to run us off. Then we moved to 86th and Lexington. Sometimes we had police protection, but we had to pay for it.

Every day for a week and a half we skipped school to man our corners. It was dangerous work, but we sold lots of papers and made lots of money. Every day one of us got beat up by the union goons. They even set our papers on fire. That was just part of the job.

My turn came to get torched. Two gorilla goons approached me, one held me down while the other one poured oil on my stack of papers. As it turned out, the one holding me down unintentionally did me a favor and taught me a lesson in marketing.

"Hey dumb kid, whatcha selling your papers for?" he jawed while I was squirming to get loose.

"Fifteen cents, wanta buy one?" Smart mouth me thought that was a good markup since I got them for three cents each.

"Sure, I'll take ten and go sell them for a dollar apiece!" They had a good laugh as his cohort put a lighted match to the oily papers and started an inferno.

I learned American enterprise at a young age. I was around ten years old.

Soon after, Pop assigned me to a new job, this time without pay. I became my sister Mary's escort. She was a teenager now, and she was pretty, shapely, and girlishly naive. She was not allowed to walk out the door unless I tagged along. This was a very boring job. I considered

Mary and our girl cousins to all be dumb. 'I thought this because they were, after all, girls. The only thing I really enjoyed was going to the street concerts when a young, skinny Italian singer by the name of Frank Sinatra performed. The mob of silly screaming girls fainted, drooled, swooned, with some throwing their underwear at him. It was kind of fun, the uproar. At least the music was top notch, very danceable. I didn't mind dancing with those weird silly girls.

Poor Sis. Without me she went to Florida with our girl cousins, met a handsome young airman, ran off and married him, and never came back to New York. He was her first and only boyfriend. Unfortunately, he turned out be an uneducated alcoholic. I was told she did it to get away from Pop, which I could certainly understand. He taught me how to work, but he was also a tyrant.

QUIPS FROM ART: Note to credit card customer center: "Your rates are too damn high. That's why I'm paying the account in full and closing it." –Art Keim (Show this note to the president of the company).

Part 3:

Uncle Russell—from East Harlem to Fifth Avenue

The apartment was not quite so crowded with Sis, Ana and George gone. I was about ten or eleven years old when, out of the blue, Pop told me I was moving to a new home. Next thing I know I was packed up, driven uptown, there to meet "Uncle Russell," who I would be living with.

Nobody told me anything, except my new Uncle Russell, who said something that didn't register with me at the time, "Now you won't have to deal with Pop anymore."

A new way of life began for me. I had a speech tutor, a tennis coach, valet, all lessons preparing me for the Cotillion and assorted other social graces. Uncle Russ was a member of the New York Social Register. Every weekend we attended parties, went to the ballet, the symphony, the art museums, the yacht club, and other highbrow events.

We romped around Newport, Palm Beach, Fort Lauderdale, Havana, Banff, and Hawaii. Sometimes it was business, but most of the time for me it was play. He introduced me as his nephew. I loved my new life. There was to be no more rooftop jumping with my shoeshine brothers.

How did this happen to me? I'm sure Pop negotiated some kind of financial arrangement unbeknownst to me. I feel like Uncle Russ took care of everything on a proper legal basis, because he was a proper and successful businessman. Adoption? Legal guardianship? There was only one detail of the arrangement that I was sure of. Pop and my family were cut off permanently, totally out of my life. It didn't bother me a bit.

Many years later I found out that Russell really was my uncle. He was married to my father's sister, an older aunt who I never knew. She and Russell were both graduates of the Wharton School of Business, part of the University of Pennsylvania. They had a short marriage because she died young and left him a lonely bachelor.

Sidenote: I never knew if any of the above was true. Somehow, I doubt it.

High society has a dark side, which I felt as a newcomer, although I was groomed to act like one of them. Russell did a good job in training me socially and otherwise. There was never a problem. He was pleasant and popular. Yet I felt something was missing. What was it? Whatever whispered to me wasn't shouting.

Life was different now. Better? No, it was just different.

Russell sent me to Connecticut to a boarding school. My classmates were international, a mix much like my former street experience, though with considerably higher economic and education levels. We were buddies, young guys learning and preparing for life. From Russell I had learned a little about finance, and I created myself a job doing tax returns for my rich roommates.

I must have learned something from Uncle Russell besides finance. By osmosis, he taught me to be generous. He was a great tipper, and he always enjoyed giving away a little money. It was his nature to compliment the servers, the cabbies, the doorman, the first responders, the street urchins. He always passed along a handsome tip. Everybody was important to him, and I will always remember that. Hey! Maybe that's where he discovered me, a skinny runt shining shoes and tap dancing on Fifth Avenue with my street urchin buddies.

In my junior year two of my best friends, two brothers from Cuba, didn't show up after Christmas break. Their daddy was a diplomat. Their whole family was assassinated during the holidays by the Castro regime and the Communist takeover. I learned from this that money doesn't mean brains, happiness, safety or love. These assets are non-discriminating and are not guaranteed because you are rich.

After prep school I tried college. I was not the least bit successful. Somehow, a classroom education didn't fit me. Russell arranged an art scholarship for me at the University of Pennsylvania, which I refused. I tried Cornell University, then Rollins College in Florida, where I mostly played tennis instead of going to class. My English professor would look out the window, see me on the tennis court, and count me present.

In the U.S. Navy now

So much for a formal education. I got wind that my older brothers had joined the Navy. That's what I did. It was war time. The Navy sent me to boot camp on the Great Lakes, then on to Treasure Island, San Francisco.

I got appointed company's clerk because I could type and knew how to pack a perfect sea bag. I was also trained as a corpsman. We worked in pairs. My partner, and my best friend, was a black guy named Sam. He was smarter than me, educated, good natured, and also a Muslim. Next thing we knew, we shipped out for Korea.

When our ship, a heavy cruiser, the SS Los Angeles, got close to our destination, we got shot at by big cannons. I thought my ears would explode inside my head. We landed to evacuate the U.S. soldiers. Sam and I always stuck together as we hit the beach running. Every mission was pure bedlam with bullets whizzing too close, collectively a deafening roar of hellish terror.

I had a problem with regulations that required us as corpsmen to wear a red cross arm band and a red cross on our helmets. I refused because I considered it a target for enemy fire. It got me demoted. I suppose they still needed me, so I was allowed to continue working with Sam. We were good together. He, the faithful, obedient, rule following, perfect soldier, wore the red cross.

Too soon the unthinkable happened. It was a routine mission, dodging bullets, crawling around looking for the wounded. I heard the "pow" of rifle fire close by. I saw Sam go down. He took a bullet in the head, his helmet with the red cross blown to smithereens. It should have been, definitely could have been, me instead of him. I'm lucky it wasn't.

That really hurt deep. It still hurts. Sam was gone. My emotions were raging. I failed to notice but my ears had gone deaf from the artillery fire from both sides. The crossfire took a lot of casualties. I was not allowed to stop. I had to keep working until my commanding officer gave the signal to retreat. I felt Sam's spirit still with me though his body lay lifeless on that strange foreign beach. After an eternity the command came and with God's help we both made it back to the ship. I kept thinking of what Father Flanagan of Boys Town fame said, "He ain't heavy. He's my brother."

Things are kind of blurry after that. Somehow the military allowed me along with an officer to escort Sam's body back to his family in Florida. So ended my brief career in the US Navy.

I was around twenty-one years old.

QUIPS FROM ART: Art's favorite flower— gladiators (red gladiolas).

IT TOOK A WHILE FOR LITTLE ARTIE TO DISCOVER THAT HIS FIRE ENGINE TOY TENDED TO BE RECYCLED EVERY CHRISTMAS. LEFT: ART'S PARENT'S WEDDING PHOTO 1924, JAN. 15...CHARLES KEIM AND ALICE QUINONES. RIGHT: EVARISTO "POP" QUINONES WITH ARTIE'S MOTHER, ALICE, AND TWIN SISTER LOLA, PUERTO RICO ABOUT 1912.

Little orphan Artie, age 5, and Chief, formidable guard of Pop's illegal hooch made for the mafia. (East Harlem, NY, NY 1936)

ABOVE: ART'S BAND OF
STREET BROTHERS PLAYING
HOOKIE ON THE EAST SIDE.
ARTIE IS STANDING LEFT.
ARTIE'S OLDEST BROTHER
CHUCK IS ON THE RIGHT.

FROM TOP LEFT: ARTIE OUTSIDE UNCLE RUSSELL'S HOME ON LONG ISLAND. RUSSELL ALSO HAD TWO APARTMENTS IN THE CITY. HIS NEIGHBOR TO HIS E. 91TH STREET APARTMENT WAS BERNARD BARUCH, PHILANTHROPIST AND ADVISOR TO PRESIDENTS WOODROW WILSON AND FRANKLIN ROOSEVELT. TOP RIGHT: ARTIE AT HUNTER COLLEGE ON PARK AVENUE (HIGH SOCIETY). LEFT, UNCLE RUSSELL FIELD PRUDDEN ON HIS BOAT IN THE WATERS OF BERMUDA, 1949.

GRADUATION PHOTOGRAPH OF ART AT OLD FARMS PREPARTORY SCHOOL IN CONNECTICUT, WHERE HE WAS ALSO AN ACCOMPLISHED MEMBER OF THE SCHOOL TENNIS TEAM. LEFT: AT 20, ART DECIDED COLLEGE WAS NOT FOR HIM OPTING INSTEAD TO JOIN THE NAVY...JUST IN TIME FOR COMBAT DUTY IN KOREA AS A CORPSMAN. ART IS ON THE LEFT.

Part 4

Life on My Own

Active military days were over, although I spent quite some time in a hospital. Physically it was my ears, and I also suffered from something else they called "shell shock" in those days. Finally, they dismissed me, and I headed for Florida again. Uncle Russell had a job lined up for me.

He'd arranged for me to take care of five idle yachts in the Fort Lauderdale harbor. The absentee owners were from New York. As caretaker there wasn't much to do, just be around and keep everything clean. When spring break came, bringing with it thousands of party-minded college kids, yet the yachts were still idle, I decided to make some money by renting out sleeping space to college kids. They weren't allowed below, only on the decks. No food, no beer, allowed. Bring your own pad. Restrooms were on the dock. I had to stay up all night to maintain law and order, and to confiscate any alcohol. It was a full house every night! I was the same age as my customers. It worked out fine.

During the slow season I flew to Havana, Cuba, on weekends. I usually flew with Mackie Airlines, which offered a $49 round trip. I always had a bunch of friends go too. We stayed at the International Hotel, gambled, did the pool parties, and danced all night. I still have the bongo drum I played with the band, a keepsake from my bachelor days.

It was a regular event for me to take my friends to see "Superman." This was kind of a private sideshow featuring a guy with a "superman" penis that hung down to his knees. This was not a carnival gimmick. The always small audience was asked to remain silent, no response, no jeering, no heckling, no bravos. We saved our comments till we got outside. Years later the same guy appeared as an actor with a bit part in one of the Godfather movies. You do what you can to make a living.

Uncle Russell wanted me to come back to New York, but I wasn't ready. Instead, a wild hair told me to jump in my green Cadillac with the long fins and head for Texas. I'd discovered my middle brother, George, who I barely knew, was an engineering student at the University of Texas, located in Austin. Yes, I found him. And his wife. And two babies! Scary! This was definitely not my choice of lifestyle.

The trip was not a total loss, though. The good part was that we went to a dance party, and that's when I met Jeanette, this cute little coed beaming with a charm and self-assurance that took my breath away. I was on a mission. Don't goof up! With the arrogance of an Iberian prince, I used my best prep school manners and I approached her with a simple, life-changing request. "Could I have this dance?"

With the coolness of a Basque shepherdess, she looked me over and said, "Do you know how to dance?"

We danced a waltz on a crowded dance floor, totally lost in the magic of the moment. When the music stopped, we were the only couple on the dance floor. The others, standing around watching us, cheered and began applauding, but I didn't notice. All I could hear was Ezio Pinza belting out "Some Enchanted Evening," the lyrics seeming to be for me and me only, "Once you have found her, never let her go. Once you have found her, *NEVER LET HER GO.*"

We've been dancing together ever since.

Nine months later we had a home wedding in Jeanette's old neighborhood. My brothers George and Chuck attended. We had a private dinner that evening, and they put us on a plane to Los Angeles. Next morning, I went to work at the dance studio. So began our lives together.

Like most marriages that last, we weathered the ups and downs. The record shows, we took the blows, and we survived. It's been good. That's the story of love.

QUIPS FROM ART: Note from Art responding to a wedding invitation: "Here's a hundred bucks. If you get divorced, I want it back."

Art and Jeanette on their wedding day

Jeanette and Art celebrate their 50th outside the UT Tower

Open House

1419 Lipscomb Street
Fort Worth, Texas 76104

Saturday, November 27, 2004
2 pm - 4 pm

You are invited to an open house and reception
honoring
Arthur & Jeanette Keim
and
Deanna Crook

The house at 1419 Lipscomb was built in 1907 by Jeanette's grandfather, Frank Stearns.
Jeanette's father, Harry and Jeanette grew up there. On Sunday, September 8, 1957 Jeanette and
Arthur exchanged vows in a home wedding in the living room. Deanna Crook, the present owner,
restored the house to its present condition.

Please honor us with your presence.
At 3 pm there will be a renewal of vows. The Rev. Scott Wooten officiating.
RSVP the Keims (817) 626-5329
(No gifts please)

Jeanette and Art's renewal of vows celebration.

ART WAS NEVER RISK-AVERSE, AND ALSO ALSO FREE WITH HIS POLTICAL OPINIONS, SOMETIMES IN VERY VISIBLE WAYS. THIS WAS TRUE WHETHER IT WAS TRIMMING HIS OWN TREES AT CONSIDERABLE HEIGHTS, OR PROTESTING WHAT HE SAW AS AN INAPPROPRIATE SELECTION OF A PRESIDENT.

ABOVE: ART AND JEANETTE ENJOY AN ORDINARY DAY WITH THEIR
GRANDSONS, JACOB AND REECE, AND SISTER MARY.
BELOW: ART MADE NO SECRET OF HIS POLITICAL SENTIMENTS.

Ever the entertainer, Art charms at the Milan
Gallery in downtown Fort Worth (about 2000).

(Photograph by Rosie Steinman, Fort Worth Sokol)

<u>Part 5</u>

Witch Hunt Melodrama

Art Keim vs The Church

Now in our later years we've had a surprising episode that, and yes, we survived, but it took its toll. For others who have been through the same thing, or something similar, keep the faith! Trust in God's timeless judgement. The bad guys will get their just due. An old Spanish proverb says that God always finds a way to make man's sins his own punishment.

This is what happened to us with excerpts from Jeanette's journal ...'

Art Keim vs the Church

Fire of fear, fueled by frauds, fanned by fanatics,

Fight on, fight on, It's funny! (Circa 2014-15)

I gave cash money to children at church who participated in the worship service in special ways. One family, whose father was a lawyer, reported to the pastor that I scared his daughter. I do remember one incident involving the child. I remember giving her and her younger brother both a $10 bill in the presence of their grandmother.

Through the years I gave lots of cash away—to children, teenagers, missionaries, college students, guest speakers, etc. etc. No one told me that giving cash away to someone at church is socially unacceptable nowadays. I never tried to hide it. There were always witnesses around. Nobody ever refused my gift.

What is going on? Maybe church leaders didn't know my background or where I was coming from. During my childhood, I received gifts and money from generous souls. It made them happy, and it made me happy. I always wanted to be kind; the way adults were kind to me. I always thought it was good to be thoughtful and giving, an act of gratitude from my heart. Uncle Russ taught me to be generous and I wanted to be like him.

The pastor called me into his office and told me to stop giving money away. The conversation came to a screening halt when I noticed someone moving behind the drapes. I saw their shoes. Who was this? A secret witness? A bodyguard? I told the pastor that the conversation was over, and I left. What was left behind was a nasty rumor that Mr. Art was a predator, and according to the church lawyer, "It (the church) takes the safety and security of church members and guests very seriously."

That's how it started. No one from the church ever asked me about anything, no inquiry, no discussion, no defense to the allegations. Their minds were made up. The church has a predator on their hands! This amounted to kindling an invitation to hysteria, without evidence, with no proof, no investigation, no facts, only hearsay, escalating rumors (the sky is falling), the church apparently but firmly believed that Art Keim was guilty. We say so. This is what we want to believe. Fanning the fire of unfounded fear, the leadership of the church became the judge and jury. A real judge hears both sides of a case before judging and punishing. Not this church!

The assistant minister kindly asked me to stop giving away cash to children and give it to the church, and they would pass it along to the children. I agreed. But I also stopped giving money, period. Still, I continued to serve the church as deacon, usher, and greeter. It was my pleasure to visit the hospitals and nursing homes on Sunday afternoons as always. This was my way to serve the Lord.

Like the red letter "A" for adulterer in Nathaniel Hawthorne's, "Scarlet Letter" two centuries ago, the church hung a purple "P" around my neck. The difference is the accusation was in secrecy, the purple "P" invisible. Punishment, or I should say black balling, followed.

I was totally unaware that there was a problem. Instead of confronting me at the time of his deep concerns, the fearful lawyer father took his grievances to the pastor who dropped the term, "predatory behavior." So began the church's unfounded suspicion that they had a child abuser on their hands. They took action via undercover, secret surveillance, tailing my whereabouts at church, seeking evidence. By law, institutions, schools, churches, etc. are required to report any sign of child abuse to the authorities. The church didn't go that far. This was because in truth they had nothing to report. Instead, they became a self-appointed posse of vigilantes.

So began the fear factor in high gear. It's funny now, but at the time I was innocently naive and didn't recognize or suspect what was going on. The church had secret spies watching my every move and reporting it. This included staff, and two lay committees of about twenty-four members each. I never had a clue! They were on a mission to nail a child abuser. He gave money to children! Could be predatory behavior. In their fearful eyes, Art Keim was guilty. We say so.

> **False fears are foes.**
> **Truth tatters those**
> **When understood.**
> **--Mary Baker Eddy**

Approximately two years later, Summer/2017

I sent that same child a postcard from the church wishing the summer campers a pleasant week. I selected her card from a big stack of cards because I recognized her name, and I didn't recognize any other names. Based on the postcard the fearful family reported to the church that Art scared their daughter again. The family never reported anything negative to me. I saw them every Sunday they attended. Greetings were always mutually friendly.

> **Truth comes with enemies.**
> **(From Don Quixote, Cervantes)**

Spring/2018

I was called to a meeting at the church. I attended, not knowing what it the meeting agenda was. They presented me with a letter unsigned by the typewritten names of the Chair of Elders, Associate Minister for Youth, Chair of Worship Life Committee, and Vice Chair of Elders. Big titles! Important church leaders. Here comes the punishment.

The above church committee listed that

--Art Keim would only attend the 11 a.m. service

--Enter and exit through the front doors only.

--Was not allowed in any part of the church except the sanctuary,

--Would stay away from the fearful family.

I was told to sign. I refused and added, "I want to talk this over with my wife." Which I did. In response Jeanette fired off a letter to the church leaders the same day.

"Now you are hearing from Art's wife. His signature is not a statement of consent to the terms. Art went to the meeting today not knowing he was on the defense. What is the accusation? What is the evidence? Art is an innocent victim of this issue.

This is a witch hunt. We are not lawyers. In Art's defense he has never touched a child, female or other, at church or anywhere else. He's been known for giving money to children, youth, and adults at church on special occasions for events such as graduation, baptism, etc. No one ever refused his gift. He thought it was an act of love, in recognition for their achievement.

The terms of this edict are malicious and made to injure. Defamation of character has been inflicted on my husband by a band of vultures."

God knows. (Jeanette Keim)

"Be careful in slaying the dragon that you do not become the dragon." (Nietzche)

Two weeks later I was called to another meeting. There was a discussion, the committee claiming that a child's safety was the issue. I felt under duress and reluctantly signed but not admitting guilt or misconduct. I really thought by signing I was showing willingness to cooperate with their demands. I immediately sent a handwritten apology to the fearful family for any problem I may have caused.

I obeyed the restrictions for about 10 weeks, then attended the 9 a.m. service thinking I had served my unstated time. While I was sitting alone in the pew, the vice chairman of elders appeared, grabbed my arm and told me to leave. I told her to get her hands off me because she was looking for trouble. She said she would go outside and get the policeman directing traffic to come and arrest me. She stomped outside. The policeman refused to leave his post. She returned and sat behind me till the service was over. She then followed me to my truck.

Looking back on it, now I can forgive her for her heated, unjustified actions. This upstanding church official was simply doing her duty, trying to deter a criminal, not an alleged criminal, but a guilty child abuser. After all, I violated their rules. According to their rules I was only allowed to attend the 11 a.m.. service.

July 10, 2018 early evening - Jeanette's Journal entries

Past Chair called to speak with Art. I (Jeanette) answered the call. He refused to explain the nature of the call and Art refused to come to the phone. I told the caller, "Art is not discussing anything with you or the church until the committee puts in writing what are the charges, what is the penalty, and what is the time limit. Then Art will have material for his lawyer." The Past Chair said he would get back with us.

Time dragged on. Four months rolled by, but still there was no word from the Past Chair. When autumn rolled around, Jeanette sent a reminder letter to the Church. We, the family of Art Keim, would like some closure to this bitter and lingering issue. We are of the opinion that our church is practicing elder abuse (Signed by Jeanette Keim).

In late autumn, November 25, 2018, Sunday morning to be exact, Jeanette answered a surprise phone call from the fearful father. By then his fearful daughter was a teenager. According to Jeanette it seemed to be a friendly call: he casually mentioned information that we were not aware of, surprising news to us. According to him, his family never received my handwritten note of apology in May. (I copied the same note over again and mailed it on November 26, 2018, the next day.)

Mr. Fearful stated that he complained to the church over three to four years ago that my giving money to his children was unacceptable. He claims that when his daughter sees me, it upsets her. To be a good parent, Mr. Fearful said he thought the church needed to take action.

My wife asked him why he didn't tell me face to face of the situation. After all he ushered with me every Sunday.

His answer, "I was afraid Art would cause a scene and embarrass me or hit me."

He told Jeanette the Church has been tracking me for a long time and telling his family when I was nearby so they could sit somewhere else to avoid me.

(Talk about passing the buck. Where was this guy's parental responsibility?)

November 29, 2018

Letter from church elders finally stating alleged charges in writing: To protect the safety of children.

Penalty: Banned from church except the 11 a.m. service, with an indefinite time limit

Checking the closeness of the dates between the phone call and the "alleged charges in writing letter," we assumed the church and the fearful family had been in cahoots continually for a number of years. We were unsuspecting the whole time. My street smarts didn't kick in this time.

Sunday—March, 2019, 10 a.m., Sunday School Class: Staff members spoke on behalf of the Church: according to some who were present the prepared message left the impression that Art Keim's behavior at church could be considered "grooming children" for predatory intent.

This was more fanning the fires of fear with no opportunity for rebuttal! My giving of money stopped nearly three years ago. There was to be a continuation of punishment involving more probation for a minimum 5 months, maximum 6 months. Then I can return to church and attend my Sunday School Class but must be escorted to the sanctuary by a class member. Jeanette and I have been active members of this church for around 50 years. Many of our class friends had died off, moved away, or changed churches because things change with time. The ranks were thinning. Our generation was being replaced by younger people who think differently. We don't understand this fear factor. To us, faith and fear are contradictory. How could a church family punish one of their own on such flimsy concerns without so much as an inquiry?

We do great damage to each other when we operate from a place of fear and prejudice. (Pre-justice, pronounced differently, is another way to say prejudice.)

What happened to independent thinking? Hear both sides of an issue? Just maybe there is no issue.

The church staff, the elected church officials, the Fearful Family, my church friends who didn't come to my defense, those who remained neutral or unassuming; a host of sanctimonious Pharisees don't have a clue to the deep hurt and heartache they caused and perpetuated. Not a clue. Not a care.

Open minds? Loving hearts? Lord, help us to be what we say we are.

This whole melodrama lasted nearly four years. The church kept things mostly hush, hush, underground. Many of our church friends, old and new, never had an inkling of what I was dealing with. Occasionally someone noticed that I wasn't around much anymore, but nobody said a word of inquiry. God bless the few, a handful of faithful souls, who were interested in my wellbeing, and had the courage to stand by me no matter what. They are my heroes forever.

I admit I did my share of misbehaving. I was a wounded tiger. My shut-in friends who watch the service on TV told me they looked for my now white hair on the front row every Sunday. There I sat, waving my church bulletin from another church in the pastor's face. I upstaged him during the recessional by dancing down the aisles which got televised. I also called the wimp pastor a son of a bitch, to his face of course.

Later, I apologized and asked for forgiveness. No surprise that my request was denied. Instead, I was slammed with more punishment. They didn't go so far as to kick me out, which I probably deserved. I was banned from the front row. I could only sit on the back pew out of range from the TV cameras.

All I wanted was exoneration. My attempts at defense were ignored. My lawyer thought it would make great headlines, this combination of elder abuse, age discrimination, defamation of character, suffering and pain, false accusations, unrelenting hostility, and documented physical abuse from the overly zealous vigilantes. My view was, "These are my Christian brothers and sisters, I don't want to start a public smear campaign. If they don't like me, and they can't deal with me, it's their problem, not mine. God knows I am innocent. I am not and never was a pervert. I accept God's judgment."

You are better acquainted with me now than any of those church folks. Yes, I am guilty of causing a three- or four-year uproar. I have to admit the shenanigans were great fun. I knew it was a losing battle. Maybe they thought I would roll over and die. The church had a mindset right from the very beginning; the church leaders, those in authority, believed that I was a predator, and nothing was about to change their minds. Art Keim's behavior could be considered "grooming children" for predatory intent. Guilty because we say so. Without any fanfare Jeanette and I joined another church. What peace we have found! God is good!

No more dodging the lances of the Don Quixotes chasing windmills. It wasn't easy cutting ties with my traditional place of worship for more than half my life. But times change. Resistance doesn't work. These days kids rule! Get used to it.

I was hoping for mercy, for a loving spirit of conciliation. This never happened. It was time to move on. Don't let your enemies take space in your mind. If something unfair happens to you in your life, and it happens to all of us, keep the faith and carry on. Remember Art Keim. He put up a good fight, he laid down to bleed a while, and he got up to fight again! That's me. I am a happy warrior for truth and justice.

May God be gracious to you on your life's journey. Enjoy every day. It's called the present, the now, a gift from God, our Maker. (Remember to say thanks.)

Slum Lord, oh yes! World's greatest dancer, oh yes! Playboy, oh yes! Child abuser, never! Bitter old man, never. Rugged individualist, oh yes! God fearing American, oh yes!

It's carved in stone on my already paid for and in place tombstone,

"WORLD'S GREATEST GRASS CUTTER,

SLUM LORD, AND DANCER"

Let's enjoy this life together.

When you're smiling, the whole world smiles with you.

Smile for Jesus. Amen. (Art Keim)

Encore

Aunt Lola and Uncle Raymond:

Before Aunt Lola passed away, Jeanette and I took a trip to New York City; Avon, Connecticut; and an upstate nursing home near Fishkill, New York, where Aunt Lola resided. It was a joyful visit with my mother's twin sister who was now over 90 years old. She was still witty and cheerful like always. We visited in a large ballroom where beautiful, recorded music was playing. No one was there but us. We talked and talked and talked.

After a while she said, "Artie, get up and dance." And we did.

When the song was over, we stopped. Aunt Lola was in some sort of trance. Finally, she said, "I just saw my brother Raymond dancing. It was so beautiful. I was in another world watching him dance again." Then she added in a faraway voice, "I will see him again soon."

Too soon. Aunt Lola died a short while after our visit. Uncle Raymond had passed away suddenly of tuberculosis during a pandemic many years ago. During his abbreviated life he was a professional adagio dancer, young, handsome, and in his prime.

***

When child abuse versus the Catholic Church made front page headlines, Jeanette and I saw a documentary about the news reporter from the Boston Globe who brought the scandalous issue to world attention. From my childhood experience, the crime was very real and truthfully familiar. However, it played out in a very different way in New York City when I was growing up. It wasn't much of a problem. Nobody reported anything; it didn't make the headlines. I personally was never abused, nor experienced anything close to it.

Jeanette asked me what was this all about. The scandal was worldwide. Why wasn't it much of an issue in New York City? I had never given it much thought, but I did have an answer.

"Simple," I began. "The Italians are Catholics. They support the churches. Ok, some little wop kid gets approached by a priest, the kid goes home and tells his daddy. If it happens again, or maybe some other kid tells their daddy the same story, next thing you know that priest disappears. A week or two later, there's a short notice in the newspaper that an unidentified male body turned up in the East River with his feet set in concrete. End of problem. The church didn't report a missing priest. Nobody said anything. The parishioners kept quiet, kept coming to church, kept giving their money, no more problem. That's how things got settled in New York."

QUIPS FROM ART:

Jeanette: "Give me some money to treat Kyla and Marsha to lunch."

Art: "No."

Jeanette: "Why not?"

Art: "I'm not paying for anybody's lunch unless I can sleep with them."

See
yourself
at the
Kimbell

kimbellart.org

FREE ADMISSION

ALWAYS SUPPORTERS OF THE ARTS, ART AND JEANETTE FOUND THEMSELVES FEATURED AS BILLBOARD BUDDIES IN A 2010 KIMBELL MUSEUM BILLBOARD (ABOVE).
LEFT: THROUGHOUT HIS LIFE, ART REMAINED A FLASHY, IMPECCIBLE DRESSER WITH A PENCHANT FOR PATRIOTIC FLOURISHES.

"SAY, DO YOU HAVE CHANGE FOR A MILLION?" NOT SURPRISINGLY, NO ONE WAS EVER ABLE TO CASH ART'S MILLION DOLLAR BILL: LEFT: VISITING UNCLE RUSSELL IN NEW YORK, ABOUT 1958.

Part 6

Slum Lord's Wife: Jeanette's Story

Meet Jean, Jean, the Piano Machine

The title of this book could easily have been "In God We Trust". That is the un-spoken given throughout Little Orphan Artie's life and our life together. We didn't verbalize much about religion. We just lived it.

Being a slumlord was not a negative in our minds, because Art provided homes to people of limited means who needed a clean, safe place to live that they could afford. Art respected his tenants, and that is why they respected him. Difficulties did arise, mostly with the authorities, city code enforcement, zoning, bankers, etc.—people in power who never owned a rent house and never dealt with the underprivileged, eyeball to eyeball.

Art understood his tenants and was successful at it. He by nature practiced "love your neighbor as yourself" and didn't even know it came from the Bible. He was just doing what, for him, was doing what comes naturally.

Life with Art. We had sixty-three years together and it was good. Not every moment, but it was a time of permanence. Good or bad, we belonged together. We gave our commitment to God in marriage that we would stick it out "till death do us part". That's what we did.

How did I choose him? He was different from the Texas boys I grew up with. Yes, he was handsome, charming, intelligent and cultured, but the strongest appeal was love.

I can't exactly explain it. I didn't chase him down—he picked me too. He had my heart, and I had his from the beginning.

My criteria for choosing a lifetime mate was threefold. Can he catch a fish? Can he clean a fish? Can he cook a fish? Yes, yes, yes. He passed all three of my requirements, plus he had much more to offer. So, here we went only eight months after we met, planning a wedding. We both wanted to commit to God, the world, and each other that we belonged together forever. It takes courage to get married, so you better know what you're getting into. In the heat of romance, it's hard to think straight, and honoring a lifetime commitment is serious business. Working together as life moves forward, this togetherness is the best way to live, especially with someone you love. Marriage is God's way. It has worked for eons in the history of mankind, and that's why marriage really works better than anything else.

Me, I was a music student in college when we met. He was roving, had New York license plates on his big green Cadillac, was unattached and visiting his brother George in Texas. We were at a dance, and as we danced our first dance together, little Cupid shot us both with his arrows. Metaphorically speaking.

Poor George, who was also a student, had a wife, two babies, and a house provided by his in-laws. Art and I weren't ready for that particular lifestyle, but marriage was not out of the question. Within a few months we were married. Art had already landed a job at a dance studio in Pasadena, California.

I knew he had a little savings, but what I didn't know was that on his way to the west coast he stopped in Las Vegas and gambled away his five-digit savings. Later on, he told me he wanted to level the playing field financially before starting our life together. No help from in-laws, no obligations, and no debts either. That's what happened. We started out together penniless. Yes, that could have been, should have been a red flag. Somehow at that time in my life I never objected; never gave it a second thought. Was this naïve? Probably so, but I had faith in myself and faith that God would take care of me, so not to worry. We were happy.

Remarkably, we both had dance jobs! But it was only a fling. Pasadena was too close to Hollywood. I hated the Hollywood rat race, the self-centered, nasty people, the immorality, and the anything goes attitude. It was a world of brutal cut-throat competition with a total disregard and lack of respect for others.

I did okay and won some trophies. My stage name, which I picked, was Miss Stern, which translates to star in German. I was/am a star. My Daddy told me I was star when I was little. He said all God's children were stars. My Mama told me I was a brat. Who was I to believe? That was an easy one. I knew the answer early on. I was a star.

When I was around three years old, I remember, after playing in my sand box, mama would put me in a wash tub on the porch to wash off the sand before letting me in the house. On one occasion the phone rang inside, and she stepped away. What an opportunity! I jumped out of that washtub stark naked and ran down the block to our neighbors' home who had a PIANO! Being a hot summer day, their front door was wide open, I ran inside, pounced on the piano bench and began singing and banging on their big upright piano.

Old Mrs. Boggs (she looked like Popeye's girlfriend, Olive Oyl) came to the parlor door smiling. Then Mr. Boggs joined us. He looked like Santa with long white beard, little round glasses and a fat belly. He was always cheerful. I had an audience! The singing and banging got louder. The smiles got bigger.

Then catastrophe hit! Here came mama, yanked me off that piano bench and gave my naked bottom a whupping. She dragged me home, me kicking and screaming bloody murder, mostly because the show was over. So ended my first public performance, which I still remember.

A few months later a moving van pulled up to our house and delivered a big upright player piano. It was a hand-me-down from my Aunt Ola, Mama's sister. Cousin Robert Wayne had carved the letters C, D, and E on three ivory keys, but in the wrong place. It didn't bother me a bit. I knew what middle C was supposed to sound like. This middle C was one whole step off, so that how I got acquainted with transposing at an early age.

But back to the newlyweds in Hollywood. Art fit in better than me. I was doing reasonably well—let's say I was tolerated, barely—but my soul yearned for something more meaningful. My cohorts were long legged ex-Vegas showgirls with fake boobs, fake teeth, fake smiles, and snarly attitudes. Me, I was just a flat chested twig. Art and I agreed. Time to go back to Texas. I returned to school. We had saved some money, and Art started his ice cream business with a brand-new truck and a new business concept for Fort Worth, soft ice cream and other treats like hot dogs delivered to the neighborhoods, work sites, and special events.

Things went smooth for a while. I got my master's degree from the University of Texas. Meanwhile, Art was doing great and bought a second truck. That's when the Restaurant Association took him to court for "disturbing the peace" with his music boxes. The outcome was that his hours of service to his customers were so restricted it put him out of business.

He served the best ice cream anywhere, and the hot dogs were fresh, hearty, top quality, always hot off the grill. His product was not the issue. He passed all the sanitation inspections with flying colors. The bottom line was the Restaurant Association didn't want him on the streets competing. Food trucks nowadays are in vogue, considered campy and seen everywhere, but Art's was the first, and it took a long while for the concept to be accepted in Fort Worth, Texas, where the West begins.

The thing about Art was how he could bounce back when he met defeat. It always hurt, but he could have been a modern-day role model for the ancient Scottish tribute to the wounded warrior, "He got wounded, laid down to bleed a while, and got up to fight again."

I greatly admired his courage. When he got in trouble, which happened a lot, it was usually because he was ahead of the times—an innovator without the limits of emotional reservation. Setbacks didn't linger. He lived with ever-present faith in God, which gave him faith in himself.

Here's one tip I want to pass on to young folks and especially newlyweds. People, even strangers, often asked me this: How did Art and I manage to stay together? What was the secret of our success?

Here's my answer. The givens are love and trust in God and trust in each other. The biggest source of difficulty is usually money. That's MONEY! capitalized with an exclamation point. Manage what you have diligently. Avoid credit and credit cards like the plague. How did Art pay cash for that new ice cream truck? Remember we started out from scratch. Our pockets were empty. What did we do? We planned and saved!

We had a policy and stuck to it. Don't buy anything until you have the cash to pay for it. Student loans are killers. Financial loans of any kind can stifle your future. Doing without is not so bad. Paying cash feels good. Bargaining with cash in your hand can get amazing results. I love Mercedes cars but negotiate so relentless the local Mercedes dealership bestowed me a name of which I am proud, "Miss Pirate."

The gypsies and other immigrants—legal and illegal. especially the Asians--get by on a cash basis in this land of opportunity. No bank accounts. They work hard and respect the hard-earned money they manage to save. The magic word is management. Write it down. Keeps records. It's called a budget. Don't spend more than you earn. Stick to it. In the business world, accounts receivable should always be greater than accounts payable. That's how you build up savings! It works! A marriage is more likely to succeed when finances are not a disaster.

In God We Joyfully Trust.

Art loved going to church. It didn't matter what kind of church if it was about God, creator of the universe, be it Christian, black, white, Catholic, Protestant, Jewish, Holy Roller, Muslim, Hindu, etc. He loved them all. He didn't pay any attention to their differences. "In God we trust" was his life's motto. He found God's presence in his everyday life, and any church claiming to serve God was an okay church with him.

I wasn't stuck on any one brand of church either. So, we always went somewhere to church together. We did affiliate (join as tithing members) early on in our life together to a Christian Church. We considered this as a way of service to the Lord, Jesus Christ.

Unfortunately, in later years the Church did not approve of Art's behavior because fear overtook reason. Soon we attended another church and took our tithes with us, because they welcomed us with unconditional love. Praise God! What a joy!

It was hard to leave so many loyal friends, but they are still our friends in Christ forever. Art was at peace to leave the final judgement and punishment, if any, in the hands of God. I was the one that expected justice now, but that was a dead end. Nothing was going to change the minds of the church officials.

So, it's best to just move on. Art took the defeat in stride. Win one, lose one.   Trust in God. Faith conquers fear. God's justice will prevail in God's good time.

As a child, Art had received money, candy and favors from the benevolent people of New York City including Mayor Fiorello "Little Flower" La Guardia, ranked in the top three most famous mayors in America's history. Art had no clue that nowadays giving money to children was considered suspicious—as in grooming for predatory intent. A fearful father complained to the church.

In a personal conversation with the fearful father, I asked him why he didn't take his concerns to Art instead of complaining to the then pastor. After all he saw Art every Sunday morning when they ushered together.

His reply was, "I was afraid Art might hit me in the face."

There is the issue. Fearful father.   Then he complained that his child was "afraid of Art."   Wonder where the daughter got that idea? She never showed any signs of fear or concern in Art's presence and the presence of witnesses when she accepted his gift.

Fear is contagious and should be, but only if there is a reason to be afraid. Suspicion feeds on itself. Facts really matter. No church official ever interviewed Art to gather any facts from his prospective. There is more than one reality—more than one way in seeing things. They had no clue where Art was coming from, and he had no clue where their thinking was coming from.

In his mind and upbringing, giving money to anybody was a good thing. Growing up he had been a recipient of the generosity of many kind souls. Now it was his turn to give back and that made him happy. In the church's modern view, giving money to children was a sign of predatory intent. Period. Art was a threat. The witch hunt was on.

The church stood by its arbitrary position that Art's behavior could be considered predatory, and his presence at church was a danger to children. Early on a church official did ask Art to stop giving to children, or anybody, but donate to the church and they would give it in his name. He immediately stopped his giving. But the fear had already spread like wildfire. The witch hunt was on!

The church acted with punitive punishment, secret surveillance, rules of where he was allowed to sit in church, walk in the halls only with escorts, and so forth. This continued for more than two years.

Finally, Art had enough when an ice cream social we attended turned ugly, unbeknown to us. It was our Sunday School class annual event, and we were there with friends. I had a good time visiting with classmates I hadn't seen in a long time. Then it was time to go. Art and the couple we came with were not to be seen.

I casually said, "I'm looking for Art." I found them waiting for me in the hallway. They were together the whole time, and we left. I was the one that got separated. We went home thinking we had a nice evening with our friends. Not so.

This is how the church vigilantes interpreted the situation. A few days later we got a letter in the mail dated October 11, 2019, from the church stating that "On October 6, 2019 Art left the fellowship hall on Sunday evening during a church class ice cream social. His chaperones (Who? I was not a designated chaperone) had no knowledge of his whereabouts and spent several minutes searching for him. At that time youth groups and college groups were meeting in the building. Could be danger.

Danger?

No one from church asked us anything. Their minds were made up and they didn't need any information from us. Case closed.

"Vengeance is Mine, I will repay," says the Lord (Deut. 32:35 and Romans 12:15). Art was ready to let God's timeless judgement prevail in determining guilt and punishment. It was useless to buck their closed system of thinking. We walked away cheerfully from our church of over sixty years, rejoicing that God is merciful, loving, and forgiving. Art amazed me that he had no regrets. He was just happy to get rid of a close-minded church.

Art, ever an observant person, in his view thought he had seen inappropriate behavior from some of the people involved, but on those issues never said a word about these things to anybody. Was this a long-standing response ingrained in Art as a street urchin? The one that says, "Never rat on your brothers."

Same deal with the fearful parent. He was the one afraid of Art, and he actually told me so on the phone, and I quote, "I was afraid Art might hit me in the face." Why? I knew Art for 63 years, and I never saw him hit anybody in the face.

Art's response was silence. He certainly didn't air his concerns to anybody at church.

He stuck to his street urchin code of ethics, "Never rat on your brothers."

Next thing we knew, Art was under suspicion with trumped up concerns from the church officials. Was it a cover-up? It never occurred to me, nor Art, that someone may have had reason to be afraid of Art. Why? Because Art knew too much? Regardless, that someone did a great job convincing the church that Art was an imminent problem. The fire was on!

Our children are at risk! Art Keim "could be" a predator. The fire raged on and on! Finally, Art walked away from the whole matter. That took some courage! Holy boldness. Faith, not fear. He left judgement and/or punishment in God's hands. In God we trust. Art and I learned a hard lesson. Actions have consequences, even when you act in good faith.

Let go. Let God.

We do great damage to each other when we operate from a place of fear and prejudice. (Vince Gill)

Art's Boy Scout Prayer before every meal:

Thank God for this Food which we take,
Make us good for Jesus' sake.
Troop 661, 1944, NY, NY

Part 7

The Last Chapter: Retirement

After our fiftieth wedding anniversary we started looking at slowing down, viewing it as some sort of retirement for our later years. A high-rise overlooking the Trinity River was our choice. We moved in the second week after it opened for occupancy.

Sure enough, Art got in trouble the first week we were there. I thought it was funny, but the management didn't. It was late evening and Art decided to go to the pool for the first time. The lights were on, the place was deserted. He had it all to himself. Art took off his clothes and jumped in the sauna naked. It was a great moment when suddenly sirens went off. Art never realized that he was the source of the problem. Next thing he knew a female security guard came bursting in with her hand over her eyes and told him to get out and put on his clothes.

The next day we got a letter from the management. Somehow his midnight visit to the pool didn't meet with their approval. Maybe somebody forgot to lock the entrance. For sure somebody forgot to turn out the lights. Maybe the management should put up some signs. I guess they never had a naked resident in the sauna before.

The second week after we moved in, Art was approached to participate in the annual fund raiser. This year it was a "Dancing with the Stars" contest.

It sounded like fun, competition, costumes, pretty partners, dance routines, big finale. He reluctantly said

"Yes" because they were desperately looking for participants at the last minute. He didn't like the idea, because the show was in two weeks, and there were lots of rehearsals and group routines to learn.

Judging was based on who got the most votes, and votes were based on who sold the most tickets. Okay. Well, the show was great. Big audience. Lots of excitement. Professionally staged. Art danced to "New York, New York" of course. His was a professional performance.

A ninety-year-old gentleman, an ex-Marine dressed in his combat fatigues, danced or let's say shuffled to "Boogie Woogie Bugle Boy." He was the winner. His daughter had purchased 600 tickets.

I danced the next year but didn't win. We loved last year's winner, and he deserved the honor.

Jeanette's Star in the sidewalk

Well, it really did happen. I have a star in the sidewalk in Fort Worth's Historic Stockyards. It's about the size of a manhole cover. This is a project of a non-profit called the Heritage Foundation and another organization called the Texas Trail of Fame. So why did they pick me?

I'm one star among many famous others—world champion rodeo riders, western movie actors, Native American tribal chiefs, Indian code breakers, philanthropists, and the like. My star says I'm a preservationist. Well, okay, I suppose I am.

What did I preserve? This is about all I can determine.

Fort Worth's Stockyards at one time in history was a booming industry. After World War II, things changed, and the Stockyards fell upon hard times, then shut down. It was a sad closing in our Western history involving cattle raising, ranching and the cowboy way of life.

After many years of abandonment, a local movement started to restore the Stockyards as a tourist destination. The original concept was to preserve its character, not exactly as a commercial tourist attraction, but as a model of how things were in its days of glory. Western movies were big in those days, and Western or at least "country Western" music was big. The public was interested in local culture and Texas heritage. Years ago, our famous local hero, the great Star-Telegram Publisher Amon Carter, gave the city a title of "Fort Worth, where the West begins." The time was right for restoration and commercial development. It took a few years, but now the Western influence can be experienced again in the Fort Worth Historic Stockyards.

I auditioned and got a job as saloon piano player in the newly restored Stockyards Hotel. It was like new. It had to be. I remember driving by there not many years before when it was a flop house. The upper hotel rooms kept the windows open, curtains tied in knots and blowing in the breeze. It took over three years to get it up to city code and open for business.

The piano was an old upright with glass front, lighted, so you could see the red, white, and blue painted hammers. To stay in character, it was slightly rinky-tink out of tune. The bar stools were saddles. The ceiling fans were run by a connecting belt like in the old days, when someone in the basement peddled on a bicycle type contraption to make the fans go.

Of course, I knew lots of traditional cowboy songs and could play in any key.

It was wild and fun. Dancing on the bar, kissing the cowboys, singing and wailing until midnight. Art didn't mind. He never complained. When he collected rent money he would barely make it home before I did. God bless him. He trusted me to be home every night a few minutes after midnight and that's exactly what I did for more than ten years.

So, what did I do to deserve a star in the sidewalk? Here's how it happened. The Stockyards Hotel became a destination for lots of important people. They sat around the old piano and had fun like everybody else.

I was good at remembering names and made everybody welcome, including the bigwigs. We had international visitors from around the world. I made sure I played something from their country, their national anthem, a folk song, something classical. I figured out that the Japanese visitors learned English singing Oh Susannah. They all knew it. And they loved singing it for the rest of us. Their accent was funny, it made us laugh. They loved making us laugh and we loved hearing them sing.

Pictures! Everybody had a camera. Pictures on the saddles, pictures at the vintage piano, selfies wearing my cowboy hat, pictures with our regular cowboy customers that were always around with spurs a jingling. I kept two big scrapbooks on top of the piano. They were full of snapshots of local patrons and foreign visitors who sometimes came maybe once a year and always checked to find their pictures in my scrapbooks.

I remember one slow late night when a couple of Stockyards bigwigs were sitting next to the piano. They were quiet and gloomy and asked for sad songs. Then they told me that Billy Bob's, the world's largest honky-tonk, was shutting down. Texas was suffering from a big oil/ and gas bust and the state's economy was sinking fast. Man! Bad news! Bad for business!

It was true. Things got a little quiet in the Stockyards, but the hotel stayed open, and I kept my job. We all had faith that good times would return. Then I found out that Cowboy Church, which met in the rodeo arena at Billy Bob's, was shut down too. Their founder had left town and returned to his home in Calgary, Canada. That sounded permanent to me. I knew that his work must continue, and that's when I decided to keep Cowboy Church alive in the Stockyards. But where? How? Help me, God!

Well, God answered my prayers. I don't remember what I did, but we, I'm sure I had plenty of help, found a location called River Ranch. It had a bad, leaky roof but the rent was free. Things fell into place fast. We started up Cowboy Church again with a noon Sunday service, and started the Cowtown Opry at 2 p.m., same location. These were the first two nonprofits in the Stockyards. That was thirty years ago and both organizations are still in business.

Now there are several nonprofits in the Stockyards, but we were the first.

I remember helping the founders of the museum, Sue and Charlie McCafferty, get their papers in order to apply for their nonprofit designation. They also have a star in the sidewalk, which they most graciously deserve. Charlie has an ancestor who died at the Alamo.

The Cowtown Opry's mission statement is "to preserve, perform, and promote our Texas music and our Texas heritage." Cowboy musicians came from everywhere to help us get started. We had a great start! Not saloon, honkytonk entertainment, but great story-telling songs from the past and present about the cowboy way and home on the range. No Nashville glitter, no sequins, no miniskirts. Just fine picking, singing, fiddling, yodeling, whistling, harmonica playing, poetry, roping, chuck wagon vittles, and living the cowboy way.

The Opry's Buckaroo program is teaching the young ones our Texas traditions. Every show opens with the ringing of the cow bell, a Texas tradition started by Amon Carter when he bought Fort Worth its first statewide radio station in 1928, WBAP. Every day the noon news opened with the ringing of the cowbell.

The cowboy way. A man's word is his bond. Old fashioned maybe, but eternal. So, these were my contributions to our Texas heritage, the Fort Worth Stockyards, and perpetuating our Texas traditions in real life.

Most of all I am proud of the many volunteers who helped along the way. I remember one event we put together, a Christmas show in the Cowtown Coliseum, for 1,200 (maximum capacity) needy children. They were bused in, fed a spaghetti dinner in waves, compliments of the Spaghetti Warehouse. George Westby, Cowboy Church pastor, did the cooking. Music was provided by the Pacesetters, a Western, gospel group from Cleburne, Texas. We had a Christmas carol singalong. The Sheriff's Posse did a flag presentation and trick riding in the rodeo arena, and the Marines Toys for Tots annual charity gave each child a toy as they boarded the buses for home. How's that for community service? And nobody got paid.

Things did not always work smoothly for the show. I will never forget one particular incident. Our emcee was a famous disk jockey that everybody knew from, of course, WBAP. The band was ready to start, and our famous DJ, the "Midnight Cowboy," showed up drunk as a skunk.

What to do! What to do! He was about to stagger up to the mike when our volunteer program director (George's sister-in-law) yanked him off the stage before he fell off. Cool as a cucumber the Pacesetters' lead singer immediately offered to emcee. The show started on time, no mumbling, no rehearsing. Things went smooth as glass like nothing ever happened.

Now you know how the Texas spirit works to get the job done. It's the cowboy way. And that's how I got a star in the sidewalk, basically by rounding up volunteers. There was always something going on—parades, special celebrations, Pioneer Days, Chisholm Trail Days, Cowtown

Goes Green Saint Patrick's Day, Forts Muster. There we were out marching and singing and celebrating. We were promoting our heritage, and it was good for business.

Together we continued to keep up the standards that made us proud.

WITH YEARS OF PLAYING IN THE STOCKYARDS HOTEL, JEANETTE BECAME ONE OF THE MOST CELEBRATED PERFORMERS IN COWTOWN. FOR HER SERVICES IN PRESERVING THE COWBOY CHURCH AND THE COWBOY OPRY, SHE HAS A TEXAS TRAIL OF FAME STAR IN THE STOCKYARDS.

Part 8

Epilogue: Crossing the Finish Line

One day Art had a premonition. He wanted to move from our apartment overlooking the Trinity River on the west side of downtown town Fort Worth. It was a great place. We had downsized two years ago. He had sold all our rent property. His clients were dwindling as they eventually sold off their undeveloped property that Art managed. He surprised me and sold "Piece of Junk," his old work truck that he loved better than me (or that was my suspicion). It was a prize for somebody, which I will never understand. It was a magnet for old farts that gathered around and told whopper stories about cattle rustlers, gun fights, saloon raids and two-legged rattle snakes. He did buy a later model but just for show. So why was he ready to move?

He couldn't really explain. Just a premonition.

Well, we looked around. Scouted around about six months and nothing suited him. One day our second daughter, Stephanie, told us she found something she thought we might like. Art had already given up looking, and said, "No." I was not ready to give up on Art's premonition, and I told her I'd like to see it. As we climbed in her Jeep Cherokee, Art changed his mind and climbed in the backseat to "go for the ride."

Footnote: I had the privilege of naming our second daughter Stephanie Christian after Saint Stephen, the first Christian martyr. Recollect that Art named our first daughter after two lady friends who befriended him during a long hospital stay due to shell shock. I got to meet them when we first married--Mildred Leinbach and Helen Fasett. They were elderly Red Cross volunteers with thousands of hours of service.

The place our daughter found was beautiful, a waterfront unit on Willow Lake not far from downtown. The location is also a reserve for migrating waterfowl. Very private, very quiet. The manager met us, and we went inside, our daughter and me. Art stayed in the Jeep.

The unit was much smaller than where we were living, which meant downsizing again, but I was impressed with everything from the floor plan and appliances to the closets. I happened to look out the deck window and there was Art down at the water's edge, under a giant ancient willow tree, just standing there surrounded by a flock of ducks.

He stood there over ten minutes, then slowly walked up the path and came inside. He went straight to the manager.

"We'll take it."

We did. We moved. It was a good move. I was nudged with little red flags now and then but didn't take notice. Why did Art give up Piece of Junk without a fight? In fact, he got rid of the new pickup before we moved to Willow Lake. Maybe he liked getting chauffeured around in my car. He drove my little sports car only one time in five years and said he hated it because it was too low and hard to get into. He said the Jeep Cherokee was too high and hard to get into. Now, he didn't mind letting me drive, even though he barked commands at me the whole time. These were red flag messages that I didn't recognize. His health was going down fast.

It was his heart, a chronic heart murmur. He had it all his life without a problem. With age the problem was escalating. An army of heart specialists told us of new surgical techniques, but they were all risky. Art said no. He preferred to live out his life on Willow Lake looking at the ducks, ducklings, long legged cranes, and noisy gulls, and that's what we did.

Our second year started out peacefully, but things suddenly turned bad in late February. A severe ice storm hit with a fury. Everything came to a screeching halt. Roads were impassable. Power lines down. Massive areas had no heat, no water, no electricity. Our close neighbors suffered broken water pipes, flood damage, no heat, but somehow we were spared. We were housebound, isolated and inconvenienced, but not suffering like so many. The grip of the bad weather held on for two weeks.

"I'm ready to go now," Art told me.

My mouth dropped. I was startled, not sure of what he meant and almost afraid to ask.

"You mean you're ready to go to heaven now? "I asked.

"Yes."

"Well," I slowly stammered, "Will you wait until God takes you?"

"That's okay." he replied.

He died exactly one week later. Peacefully. At home. He was having a late breakfast. I took him his morning medicine. He closed his eyes.

That was it.

At that point he was "Marching on To Zion" with the angels, not looking back. Let him go. My last words to him were, "I'm right behind you, Art."

He is buried in the shadows of the Amon G. Carter mausoleum, Fort Worth's great leader and innovator, the ultimate Texan. Art's tombstone says, "World's greatest grass cutter, slum lord, and dancer." My side says, "Lamb of Jesus."

To Art:

I loved you then,
I love you still,
I always have,
I always will.

From Jeanette

At rest in the shadows of the Amon G. Carter Mausoleum. Another one of Fort Worth's notable entrepreneurs.

Words of Wisdom from Art and Jeanette

We will never know all the answers but have faith that we are in the hands of One greater than ourselves. So, praise our God, our Creator of the universe. Praise his son, Jesus, who lived on the earth like us. Celebrate with us that will will rise again after this life to a better place that Jesus promised. Hallelujah!

In God We Joyfully Trust

Amon Carter Museum, 2017
"For the Joy of the Lord is our strength"
--Nehemiah

The end (but not of the memories)

Made in the USA
Monee, IL
22 January 2024

51726753R00072